CELTIC SAINTS
AND ANIMAL
STORIES

CELTIC SAINTS AND ANIMAL STORIES

A Spiritual Kinship

EDWARD C. SELLNER

Paulist Press
New York / Mahwah, NJ

Interior chapter title image by Hoika Mikhail / Shutterstock.com

Cover images: front art copyright © 2020 by Deborah Sheehy, www.deborahsheehy.com; border image by ATeam/Shutterstock.com
Cover and book design by Lynn Else

Library of Congress Cataloging-in-Publication Data
Names: Sellner, Edward Cletus, author.
Title: Celtic saints and animal stories : a spiritual kinship / Edward C. Sellner.
Description: New York : Paulist Press, 2020. | Includes bibliographical references. | Summary: "This book explores the rich tradition of the stories of the Celtic saints and their kinship with animals, revealing a new spirituality of holiness that speaks to our times"—Provided by publisher.
Identifiers: LCCN 2019022447 (print) | LCCN 2019022448 (ebook) | ISBN 9780809154579 (paperback) | ISBN 9781587688492 (ebook)
Subjects: LCSH: Christian saints, Celtic—Biography. | Human-animal relationships—Religious aspects—Christianity.
Classification: LCC BR754.A1 S445 2020 (print) | LCC BR754.A1 (ebook) | DDC 274.1/020922 [B]—dc23
LC record available at https://lccn.loc.gov/2019022447
LC ebook record available at https://lccn.loc.gov/2019022448

ISBN 978-0-8091-5457-9 (paperback)
ISBN 978-1-58768-849-2 (e-book)

Published by Paulist Press
997 Macarthur Boulevard
Mahwah, New Jersey 07430
www.paulistpress.com

Printed and bound in the
United States of America

For Andrew and Clair Linzey
and
Red, my teacher and muse

CONTENTS

CONTENTS

PREFACE

FROM ANCIENT TO MODERN TIMES, indigenous peoples have long had a deep spiritual awareness that in this world all things are related to one another and, especially, when it comes to humankind, that we are intrinsically linked with *Gaia*, our Mother Earth. As the phenomenon of "global warming" is increasingly making clear, when we harm her, we harm ourselves. Native Americans, including those who live in my part of the world, Minnesota, have long had this sense of reality and fostered it in their daily lives and spirituality. It is reflected in the Sioux Indian phrase that is said repeatedly in their ceremonies: *mitakuye oyasin*, "all my relatives," an affirmation that we are connected with everyone and everything—not only with those people who travel with us on our pilgrimage through time, but also with animals who often act as teachers, healers, and guides. This awareness was shared with the ancient Celts of Ireland, Scotland, Wales, the Isle of Man, Cornwall in England, Brittany in France, and Galacia in Spain, a perspective they passed on to those early Celtic Christians who built monasteries that eventually grew into a Celtic Church much different from the one influenced by the dominant Roman culture that arose on the continent of Europe. A sense of kinship with animals and, really, of all creation became a major characteristic of their Celtic Christian spirituality.

This book focuses on this sense of kinship as reflected in the stories of the Celtic saints. I hope that you, the reader, will begin to recognize, if you haven't already, the significance of this quality of kinship, and affirm its importance in your own life. It is an aspect of my spiritual heritage that I had overlooked in my earlier research on those saints, even though I grew up in rural North Dakota where cattle, sheep, pigs, and chickens, as well as cats and dogs, were familiar sights and, at times, intimate friends. As I have grown older, however, certain experiences have made me more aware of this kinship between humans, animals, and birds: when I observed, for example, on my first visit to Lindisfarne, the Holy Isle off the northern coast of England, the Anglican priest there communing with his dog, and how she seemed to reciprocate, the two of them sharing a secret language; how crows gathered in my neighbor's tree across the street from my home, back in Minnesota, turning it into a living mass of blackness, the day he, a man of Irish ancestry, had died; how, at my father's burial, my aunt exclaimed aloud at all the birds filling the trees and telephone lines, seeming to have come to the country cemetery to mourn my father, a man who had fed so many of them while he was alive. Also, I was raised with various puppies and dogs, my first one, Peppy, given to me by my father at Christmas when I was almost five years old, amazing me with this unexpected bundle of energy and affection. More recently, when my dear cocker spaniel, Red, died after months of lingering illness, I came to reaffirm once more how much happiness certain pets bring into our daily lives, and how, in the midst of deep grieving, Red's loving spirit still accompanies me—even though her ashes are buried in my backyard, beneath a Celtic cross, visible from my kitchen window.

When we turn to the stories of the Celtic saints, we find numerous affirmations of this spiritual kinship, and the affection found between these saints and the animals whom they loved, and who loved them. If we pay close attention, if we practice a form of meditation Buddhists call mindfulness, we can begin to learn from these stories how to better live our daily lives more compassionately toward all our fellow-earthlings, and more appreciative of what animals give us so freely and generously as guides into a richer humanity. On our own sacred journeys through time, we might begin to see both the Celtic saints whom we admire and the animals with whom we live as true soul friends leading us to a deeper spirituality. I hope you, the reader, will spend some time with these stories. Go back in memory, if you will, and recall your own experiences of loving

creatures; acknowledge the gifts that they may have given you with their love. If you are in touch with animals today, in whatever form, take time now to observe what they may be trying to teach you, providing messages and awarenesses that may enrich even more your daily sense of beauty and reasons for gratitude.

INTRODUCTION

T
O MORE FULLY UNDERSTAND and appreciate the wisdom that the stories of the Celtic saints and their animal friends provide, let us first consider the saints' ancestors, the ancient Celts, whose spiritual leaders taught them about their mystical connection with nature and with their fellow-creatures. What we find when we consider the history, culture, and spirituality of the ancient Celts is that everywhere we turn in these Celtic traditions are stories of animals.

A CELTIC PERCEPTION OF THE WORLD

In the history of Western civilization, the Celts have, until quite recently, received little attention, largely because, unlike the Greeks and Romans, they did not write anything down until the sixth century CE, when the Latin alphabet of the Christian scribes was adapted for the writing of the native Celtic languages. Before that time, all of the Celts' history, knowledge, and lore was kept alive through the oral tradition of the bards, the storytellers, and other learned members of the tribes. Contemporary archaeologists are showing, however, that, even before the rise of the Roman Empire, the Celts, a branch of the Indo-European family from which most of present-day European, Middle Eastern, and Indian races are descended, dominated the center of Europe for centuries from the Black Sea to Spain, from the Mediterranean to the North Sea and Ireland. More archaeological evidence of the Celts' talents and sophistication, such as advanced agricultural techniques, and the craftsmanship and metalwork that have survived, clearly demonstrates the scale and importance of the Celtic contribution to the formation of European civilization. The names of major cities in modern Europe, such as Paris, Milan, Vienna, London, and Berlin, trace their origin to the Celts, as do the names of such rivers as the Thames, the Seine, the Rhine, and the Danube. In England, the cities of Bath and Wells were originally holy Celtic sites where the thermal waters were used for bathing and making offerings to Celtic deities. Even the site of the beautiful medieval Chartres Cathedral in France was once a main Celtic center where their spiritual leaders, the druids and druidesses, are said to have met annually.

The precise origins of the Celtic race are unclear. Some scholars point to the area near India, while others say that Celtic civilization emerged around 700 BCE in the Hallein region of Austria where the so-called Hallstatt Culture was born. Another location, discovered by archaeologists at La Tene on Lake Neuchatel in Switzerland, points to the presence of Celts there around the early fifth century BCE. The burial mounds at both places have produced a large number of artifacts and images that reveal people who imported luxury goods, especially drinking equipment, from the Mediterranean world, and who appreciated abstract designs in their art that incorporated motifs from nature, such as animals, birds, and foliage, as well as human faces—a trait that will appear in the most famous of illuminated Christian Gospels found in the Book of Kells, created around 800 CE.

Whatever their actual geographical beginnings, the ancient Celts engaged in a great variety of occupations as warriors, farmers, adventurers, traders, and craftsmen. They were also a nomadic people, given to travel and migration. Wherever they went, they brought with them a certain *Celtic* perception of the world, reflected in their admiration for poetry and the arts; their strong sense of the intimate connection between this world and the next; their belief in the sacredness of landscape and of a communion between the living and the dead; and, not least, their veneration of nature in all its manifestations. These qualities of the ancient Celts persisted, even after the coming of Christianity.

From the fifth through the third centuries BCE, Celtic tribes moved south into northern Italy, west through Gaul and Iberia, east along the Danube into Hungary, Greece, Turkey, and across the North Sea into Britain. By about 387 BCE, they had grown so powerful that some of them sacked Rome itself, and by 279 BCE, they attacked the Greek oracle at Delphi. Much of Gaul (present-day France), before Caesar's invasions in the 50s BCE, contained Celtic tribes. Under the Roman emperors Augustus and Tiberius, the remainder of Celtic Europe was subdued. In 43 CE, the conquest of Britain was initiated, and by 84 CE, Roman armies reached northern Scotland. Only Ireland remained unconquered by the power of Rome. Due to conflicts with other tribes, including the Anglo-Saxons, who invaded Britain in the fifth century CE, and because of their own desire to be near bodies of water, Celtic tribes eventually settled in those places we now associate with "the Celtic Fringe": Ireland, Scotland, Wales, the Isle of Man, Cornwall in England, Brittany in France, and Galicia in Spain. During Christian times, monks and missionaries from Ireland and Iona, off the coast of Scotland, passed Celtic spirituality on to the Anglo-Saxons in Northumbria, or northern England, as well as the continent of Europe, especially France, Germany, Switzerland, and Italy.

THE NATURAL ENVIRONMENT OF CELTIC LANDSCAPE

The ancient Celts' daily life was lived in close proximity to nature, and their spirituality reflected what the Welsh call *hud*: a sense of wonder and awe at the divine residing in everything. Their ancestors, like other indigenous peoples, had a deep respect for nature, regarding the earth as a mother, the source of all fertility. Their spiritual leaders believed that the supernatural pervaded every aspect of life, and that spirits were everywhere: in ancient trees and sacred groves, mountaintops and rock formations, rivers, streams, and holy wells. Influenced by that ancient spiritual heritage, Celtic Christians found it natural to address God as "Lord of the Elements" or "God of the cloudy skies" or "Lord of the starry night," and to experience communion with God in their natural surroundings. In the stories of the saints, they are often found establishing their monasteries and oratories in places where the druids and druidesses had once taught and worshipped: in the midst of oak groves or near sacred springs, on the shores of secluded lakes, or on misty islands far out at sea.

Before the saints and soul friends of the Celtic Church, even before the rise of the Celts, whom later Christian generations identified as "pagan," there was the land and the ocean that borders much of it. The Celts' innate appreciation of beauty certainly had a great deal to do with this landscape: its mountains covered with forests and flowers, its tiny islands and skellig rocks off the shores of lakes and seas, the ocean water with its ebb and flow of tides. This natural beauty, wreathed so often in mists and fogs, opened the Celts, both ancient and Christian, to the realm of the imagination. It made them receptive to mysticism, poetry, and prayer, as well as to the mysterious language and images of dreams. Located as they were so close to the ocean, the lands of the Celts were watered almost daily by mists and sudden downpours of rain. This weather, which changes so quickly and unexpectedly from bright sunshine to the blackest of days, contributes to the Celts' temperament, their outlook on life, their character. Some writers have described the Celt, in fact, as "a creature of extremes; his sadness is despairing, his joy is rapture." The same changing weather may also have contributed to their penchant for telling stories. As Bryan MacMahon once said in answer to a student's query about the flood of Irish stories, "Oh, it's the rain you know. It turns one to moody reflection, and what else can you do of a long winter's night but tell stories." Certainly nature and the natural environment contributed to the writing of stories of the saints, surrounded by the beauty of nature and animals whom they identified as friends.

Anyone who visits the lands associated with the Celts would agree that they have a common landscape. Wake up in the morning and look out through the window, and, if you are near the sea, you realize how much they look alike: in springtime one sees green leaves returning to the trees, and fuchsia blossoming in rich colors of scarlet and creamy white; in summer, wild gorse bushes splash the fields and hills with patches of bright yellow, as if from the brush of van Gogh; in autumn, the tops of mountains and hills are encircled with various shades of tan, blue, and purple heather; in winter, cold rain sweeps in sheets across rugged rock formations and deserted beaches. And always there is the smell of the sea, its vast expanse of water, its ever-changing crests of waves. Ruman, a seventh-century Irish poet, refers to the beauty and power of the ocean:

> Full the sea and fierce the surges,
> Lovely are the ocean verges,
> On the showery waters whirling,
> Sandy winds are swiftly swirling
> Rudders cleave the surf that urges.

For the ancient Celts, a people who have been described in some-times highly condescending terms as "mere animists," the landscape was inhabited by multitudes of spirits and by goddesses and gods of nature and of fertility. When Christianity came to Celtic lands, this profound pagan belief in the spiritual dimension of creation was transformed into the Christian belief in the spiritual presence and ready accessibility of God, the angels, the saints, all of whom, from a Celtic perspective, were not divorced from but closely linked with the environment. A story about St. Columcille alludes to this powerful sense of spiritual presence when it relates why he loved his Irish monastery at Derry so much, located high on the hill where the city by that name was later built:

> For this is the reason why I love Derry,
> For its level fields, for its brightness,
> Because it is quite full of white angels
> From one end to the other....
> My Derry, my little oak-grove,
> My dwelling, my little cell.

For him and other Celts, ancient and Christian, landscape was both *luminous*, overflowing with light, and *numinous*, reveling in and revelatory of sacred mystery. Contrary to those of us who live in a culture that has lost its memory and seems to only value the future and the supposedly ever-changing "new," the Celts believed that the landscape itself was filled with echoes of memory, of the eternal. To them, it was immersed in the continuing presence of past lives, and alive with reflections of former times. The Irish writer John Synge alludes to this when he says that Celts believe that there is a "psychic memory" attached to the landscape and its locales.

The Celts brought this awareness to the landscape, and their attitude toward it was one of wonder and awe at its profound beauty and effulgence. Noel Dermot O'Donoghue refers to this as "Celtic religious consciousness, Christian as well as pre-Christian," in which "creation does not merely show forth God's glory," but "has its own power, its own presence, its own mystery, its own voices." Influenced by this awareness of nature's mystery, the Irish shared with their later invaders, the Norsemen, what the Norse called *utiseta*, the practice of sitting out under the moon and the stars to listen attentively to the voices of nature, to singing water and rustling leaves. As the Irish scholar John Scotus Eriugena (c. 810–77 CE) states, "Every visible and invisible creature can be called a theophany, that is, an appearance of the divine," a belief reflected centuries later in the Welsh poetry of Waldo Williams that there is an "ancient kinship of earth and heaven."

Anyone who reads the stories of the Celtic saints or visits their holy places soon realizes that the landscape is not merely "background" to the lives of these saintly soul friends, but a vital and formative presence, affecting profoundly their spirituality and their understanding of God. This theology is reflected in a medieval Irish litany to the Trinity that addresses God:

> O Creator of the elements...
> O God of the earth,
> O God of fire.
> O God of the waters of wonder.
> O God of the gusting and blustering air....
> O God of the waves from the depths of the ocean.
> O God of the planets and of the many bright stars.

> O God, creator of the universe and inaugurator
>   Of night and day.

Animals, of course, as part of creation, contributed to the Celts' sense that they too expressed the wonder of God, and their own reasons for gratitude.

In the recognition of nature's beauty in high places or ocean depths, Celts, both ancient and Christian, experienced an outright mystical connection with nature. This sense of spiritual kinship is reflected in their profound respect for the earth and the natural rhythms of body and soul, precisely because they did not see themselves as "lords" over creation, but spiritually, emotionally, and intellectually connected with it. It is found in the belief that their daily lives and work were united with their landscape, as well as with the changing seasons of the year. It is expressed, too, in their writings. Sun and moon, sea and lake, wind and fire, earth and sky all have numinous associations in early Irish and Welsh literature, especially as seen in the poetry of the nature mystics and solitaires.

THE ANCIENT CELTS' MYSTICAL CONNECTION WITH ANIMALS

This attitude of deep respect for the environment was manifest in their quiet care for all living things. As we will see in their stories, the Celtic saints seem to have had a special affinity with animals in relationships that were reciprocated: Kevin shelters in his hands a blackbird that probably sang for him; Ciaran meets a wild boar who helps him clear land for his monastery; Columcille's white horse sheds great tears at his master's approaching death. Animals are portrayed as fellow-creatures of the earth, and once befriended, they become helpers to the saints.

Like many shamans throughout history, ancient Celtic druids and druidesses knew from firsthand experience of the mystical connection between humans and animals. Animals, in fact, were considered by them as "helping spirits" who guided not only the spiritual leaders of the tribes, but also ordinary people through life's conflicts and difficulties, sometimes helping them attain a new direction in life, a new identity. Certain animals were seen as *psychopomps*, spiritual guides for the living, but also guides of souls to the place of the dead. For both the living and the dead, an animal could provide very real contact with and direction to the spiritual world, manifest in the Celts' belief in "thin places," geographical sites where a person could experience "the thin veil" between this world and the next. Celtic legends of their heroes had much in common with those found in other lands where the hero is led by animals to new geographical sites and new awarenesses. In numerous instances, helping animals not only enables a person to be transformed, but in a direct way they become his or her "double," an alter ego, another self waiting to be born. This is particularly evident, for example, in Native Americans naming themselves after animals such as Black Elk, Crazy Horse, Sitting Bull, Lone Wolf, and Kicking Bear. For the ancient Celts, not only did individual families have names of animals, such as McMahon, which translates as "Son[s] of the Bear," but a number of tribes also took the names of animals whose attributes they admired, such as the Epidii of Kintyre (Horse-People), the Lugi in Sutherland (People of the Raven), the Caerini (People of the Sheep), the Orcoi (Boar People—whose name still lives on in the Orkney Isles), Gamandrad (Stork People), and others.

The Celts' sense of kinship with animals is also manifest in the tales of their deities and heroes, most of whom had animal or bird companions, while many were also associated with shape-shifting. The ancient god Cernunnos, Lord of the Animals, was portrayed as half human, half animal, wearing on his head the antlers of a stag. CuChulainn, the Irish hero who appears in many Irish, Scottish, and Manx folk tales, was called "the Hound of Culann" and had a special and close relationship with dogs. Finn McCool, another hero and hunter-warrior of Irish, Scottish, and Manx mythology, was known as someone who would pass through many shapes of animals and birds. His wife, Sava, is part deer and part woman; the first time he meets her she is in the shape of a fawn, having been transformed by the magic of a Black Druid. Her son, Oisin, is described as half fawn, half child, his name meaning "Little Deer." (So many deer stories may be why one of the earliest of St. Patrick has him changing himself and his men into deer in order to hide from a pursuing chieftain.) The sixth-century Welsh shaman-poet Taliesin is said to have transformed himself into numerous animals, including a snake, eagle, sow, crane, cat, goat, salmon, dog, fox, and squirrel—much as the Buddha's hundreds of previous incarnations, many as animals, before his birth as Gautama.

In addition to the shape-shifting of the Celtic heroes are the numerous ancient stories of animals themselves. Wolves appear in many of these tales, for example, associated in these stories with Morrigan, the battle goddess of the Celts, as well as the Irish king Cormac MacAirt, who was kidnapped as a child and reared by a she-wolf before he was found and returned to his mother. (In the Lives of the saints, we find two of them, Ailbe, an Irish saint, and Ciwa, a Welsh saint, being suckled by wolves as children—much as the legendary founders of Rome, Romulus and Remus, were said to have been.) Deer, especially stags, appear frequently in Celtic literature, as they also do in the later stories of the saints, who are most often depicted as protecting them from hunters. Interestingly, some of the ancient Celtic stories tell of gigantic deer-goddesses, one of whose chariot was drawn by four golden-antlered deer. Pigs and wild boars in the ancient tales are often portrayed as magical beings having oracular powers with the ability to foretell the future. The most famous sow, Hen Wen (Old White One), was said to have acquired great knowledge from eating the beech nuts that fell from the Tree of Wisdom. Otters, called "water-dogs," had skins considered lucky, and were often hunted, as in the story of the hero Muiredach, who slew the King of the Otters and afterward wore its skin as a mantle that protected him.

Numerous stories of cats appear in Celtic folklore, some of them about large black cats, associated with fairies and witches, similar to those depicted today at Halloween (the feast itself originated in Ireland). In the immram story the "Voyage of Maelduin" (a predecessor of the Christian "Voyage of Saint Brendan"), the hero and his men discover on one of the islands a seemingly harmless little kitten that suddenly changes into a flaming arrow, killing one of Maelduin's men when he was about to steal a piece of jewelry. Some Celts, notably in southeastern Wales, actually worshipped a cat; and in Scotland some of the natives called themselves

"Cats." In early Irish literature, there is reference to Inse Catt, the Isles of the Cats. Perhaps the most famous of Irish cats is Pangur Ban. Cats thus were very popular among the Celts—similar to Asian people's love of them. In Japan, for example, there are many shrines and temples, even an island, dedicated to cats and cat deities, and Buddhist monasteries in Myanmar and Thailand specifically care for cats, treated as fellow-monks (as we will see was the case in stories of Celtic saints and their animal friends). Dogs too, of course, are found in Celtic stories, some of whom we know by name, including King Arthur's great hound Cafall and Finn McCool's dog Bran. Many Celtic heroes and kings include the appellation "hound," as we saw with CuChulainn, obviously showing their love of and identity with dogs. In Irish folklore, three amazing *green* dogs appear, named Fios, Luaths, and Tron (Knowledge, Swiftness, and Heaviness)—which seems appropriate on the Emerald Isle!

Birds also often appear in the ancient tales. Crows and ravens are depicted as bringers of knowledge—crows as harbingers of death, and ravens as teachers of wisdom to the druids who would watch their behavior to discern future events. Cranes were much loved by the Irish. Perhaps the most famous story is that of the Crane of Moy Leana, who, weary and lonesome, is saved by Aengus Mac Orc, doing what he could to relieve the crane's pain (much as St. Columcille would do for a poor, weary crane seeking refuge on Iona). Swans, considered by the Celts to be Other-worldly birds, also figure frequently in Celtic stories, especially those associated with the Ulster hero CuChulainn and the love-god Aengus Og. Perhaps the most famous story of swans is "the Fate of the Children of Lir," with their fate of being turned into swans by their jealous stepmother and remaining as such for three hundred years before finally returning to human form. (In the beautiful memorial Garden of Remembrance in Dublin, dedicated to those who gave their lives for the cause of Irish freedom, the sculpture depicts the children of Lir being transformed from swans into children once again.)

So many of the stories about animals in Celtic mythology show them to have special powers. The salmon was especially revered, for example, and Celts believed that if eaten, one would gain a deep knowledge or wisdom from them. As in a considerable number of myths and legends from all over the world, the Celtic hero is often portrayed in stories as being carried into the beyond or into another stage of life by an animal. The fox, the owl, the bear, the dog, and, in Hawaii, the shark are powerful and effective helpers. Celtic heroes, ancient and Christian, are shown to have a great appreciation of animals and outright love for them, whom they considered to be fellow-creatures, often acting as teachers, healers, and spiritual guides. Encounters with animal guides and spirits, Celts believed, happen at crossroads or liminal places: at twilight, for example, or deep within a dark wood, or at the water's edge or high upon a hill—in "thin places," where there appears only a thin divide between this world and the next, between past and present and future times; geographical locations where different worlds and species come together and interact for their mutual benefit. A Celtic proverb alludes to these mysterious, mesmerizing places like the windswept isle of Iona or the rocky peaks of Croagh Patrick: "Heaven and earth are only three feet apart, but in thin places that distance is even shorter."

These numerous Celtic animal stories that preceded those of the Christian saints bear witness to the central belief of the Celts that wisdom is derived from association with animals and friendship with them. It is important to place the stories of the saints and their kinship with animals in the context of these ancient stories that were being told in tribal circles and around flaming hearths long before Christianity arrived on Celtic shores. These, the earliest Celtic stories involving animals, were verbally passed on from generation to generation by the bards, the storytellers of the ancient Celts, before they were compiled and written down in the early Christian period of the sixth century by the monastic scribes.

ARTISTIC DEPICTIONS OF KINSHIP WITH ANIMALS

Fascination of and admiration for animals explored in their stories were manifested time and again in the images and symbols of animals in early Celtic art, particularly metalwork and jewelry, with bulls, boars, deer, and wolves as favorite subjects. Even here human and animal forms were often mixed in their artistry when a human face or head may have the ears or horns of an animal. Statues of Celtic divinities often show them accompanied by animals, as mentioned earlier, most often bulls, boars, deer, wolves, and horses, and birds such as the raven. This is perhaps most beautifully expressed artistically in the famous Gundestrup cauldron, created about 100 BCE, where the god Cernunnos is depicted seated cross-legged, with tall antlers on his head, while holding a giant snake in one hand and a Celtic torc in the other, surrounded by numerous animals such as stags, dogs, and even a dolphin with a human rider! Celtic iconography shows animals represented as more equal to their gods and goddesses than in Roman classical tradition, where they are always depicted as subordinate. There is, thus, in Celtic art, more a sense of mutuality and equality of nature and the animal world with the human and spiritual or divine realms—no rigid barriers between human and animal forms.

This sense of equality between humans and animals is vividly portrayed in later medieval church ruins, obviously reflecting the ancient Celts' appreciation of animals before Christianity arrived. The portal archway, for example, of a medieval monastic church at Dysert O'Dea in Ireland shows twelve human and seven animal heads intermixed with each other, obviously expressing what we today would call "cross-speciesism." On the doorway of Clonfert cathedral at the site of a monastery founded by St. Brendan in 554 CE, even more human and animal heads are visible. In another part of Ireland, at Cormac's Chapel, on the Rock of Cashel, numerous mysteriously carved heads, appearing to be both human and animal, decorate one of the archways. On a tympanum over the main door, a centaur, a mythological creature with the upper body of a human and the lower body and legs of a horse, is depicted attacking with arrows a huge lion. Again, there is this physical mixing of human and animal forms.

Reflecting this ancient Celtic appreciation of animals, numerous Christian high crosses of Ireland, Cornwall, Wales, northern England, the Isle of Man, and Scotland are filled with depictions of animals, wild and tame, domestic and foreign. There, on these distinctively beautiful stone crosses, amid multiple carvings of Scriptural heroes, from both Old and New

Testaments, as well as desert fathers and Celtic saints, animals appear. Some of the bases of these crosses show deer, ducks, dogs, and cats. Even a camel and lions—hardly common creatures in Celtic lands—are found on a high cross in Drumcliff, Ireland, depicting scenes from Scripture. Other crosses in Ireland are rich with animal scenes. On the Kells Market cross is a man bearing a long staff with a dog at his feet. Moving before him from right to left are a large bird with open wings, a frog, a fawn, a young bull, a boar, and two fine stags with spreading antlers. On another Kells cross two horsemen mounted on steeds ride before a chariot in which are two persons. A dog runs alongside. (The people or monks at Kells must have had an appreciation of dogs!) On a cross at Castledermot are figures of two men, the lower carries a spear and the upper a club, and they are hunting or herding a hare, deer, pig or boar, and a bird. At Ahenny, the site of the earliest Irish high crosses, one cross has the scene of animals that fills most of the base with a man standing under what appears to be a palm tree. Scholars interpret this as a scene of Adam in the Garden of Eden naming the beasts, since a palm tree often indicates a scene of Paradise. At Monasterboice, on Muiredach's high cross (one of the finest pieces of early medieval sculpture in Ireland) is a panel depicting two desert fathers, Anthony and Paul of Thebes (from a story of St. Jerome) holding a loaf of bread with a raven on the ground beside them. Two cats, one with a kitten, the other with a bird, sit in high relief on the lowest part of the shaft. These are just a few of the many high crosses in Ireland with animals carved on them in stone. Scotland's high crosses also have numerous animals, birds, fish, and men on horseback—as do those in Northumbria, England, the Isle of Man, and Wales.

Besides the sculptured carvings, there are the illuminated Gospel books from the later Christian centuries that are alive with animal imagery. The most famous, the Book of Kells, is now on view at Trinity College, Dublin. On its pages, amid whirls, spirals, and geometric circles, there are wrestling animals, writhing snakes, birds and fish, cocks and hens, all painted in bright colors of wine red, indigo yellow, emerald green, and deep ocean blue. The numerous illustrations of animals reveal an otter catching fish, a panther with a red tongue hanging out, cats (in individual and family groupings), mice that are tugging at or escaping with communion hosts, a hare, and, of course, a lion, eagle, and calf, representing the three evangelists of the Gospels: a lion for Mark, an eagle for John, and a calf for Luke, while a man represents Matthew. Lions in other parts of the Gospels symbolize Christ—as Aslan in C. S. Lewis's *Chronicles of Narnia* represents him. A greyhound also appears, along with a fish that resembles a salmon, multicolored peacocks, a stag, a she-goat, a dove, and a wolf. A domestic cat, its tail curled up, is depicted within the gospel pages, along with a hare that bites a vine. And snakes, a major decorative element in the manuscript as a whole! Though later synonymous with the devil, here the snake was a common symbol of Christ's resurrection from the dead. (As the sixth-century church father St. Isidore commented, "Snakes are said to live for a long time, because when they shed their old skin they are said to shed their 'old age.'") Many of these animals in the Book of Kells can also be found in two earlier illuminated gospel books, the Book of Durrow (also at Trinity College) and the Lindisfarne Gospels (at the British Library in London).

All these artistic depictions of animals reveal how much they were considered as fellow-creatures who shared a common life with humans. The properties of animals—their speed, sharp hearing, keen sight, the ability to fly for some—elevated them in Celtic eyes and caused them to be perceived as in some ways superior to humans. This attitude is found not only in the artistic ways animals were depicted from earliest times on into the Christian period, but in the Celtic stories, both ancient and Christian, where they receive such prominence. In them a peculiar rapport between humans and animals is expressed, and even a deep respect and admiration for animals having traits humans did not! This was manifest, we will see, as we turn to the coming of Christianity to Celtic lands and the stories of the saints who loved animals and all of creation as the foundation of their spirituality.

THE EARLY CELTIC CHURCH, RURAL AND MONASTIC

No one knows with certainty when Christianity arrived in Ireland, England, Scotland, Wales, Brittany, the Isle of Man, and Spain. St. Patrick is perhaps the best-known of the missionaries who converted Ireland, but he certainly was not the only saint to proclaim the good news of the gospel. Christianity came to Celtic lands by many routes, spread through the influence of many ordinary Christians. It may have come first to Gaul (France) from the Middle East, where Jesus had lived, to Rome, the heart of the Empire, where Sts. Peter and Paul preached the good news and were martyred. With the arrival of the Christian faith in Gaul, Britain, Ireland, and beyond, the Celtic Church began to flourish in the early centuries from the mid-400s on, primarily in rural areas before the rise of cities (largely due to the growth of later Viking settlements). Because of the Celtic tribal traditions, monasteries arose that became towns and cities in themselves. By 600 CE, in Ireland alone, there were more than eight hundred monasteries, and many more in other Celtic lands, all of them bordering the ocean or other bodies of water. What emerged in those lands where the Celts lived and where Roman culture and institutions were not dominant was a Christian church that functioned more like an inclusive circle than a pyramid in the way authority was used and decisions made. While the Roman church on the continent adapted the social structures of the Roman Empire by dividing land into dioceses with bishops in charge, Celtic Christians adapted their tribal structures to monastic communities, family oriented, with abbots and abbesses as spiritual leaders, some of whom were married with families of their own—with or without bishops in their midst. Celtic monasteries were linked by the friendship between their communities through their abbots and abbesses, not through the jurisdiction of a hierarchy.

While the Roman church increasingly isolated women from ecclesial positions, influenced as it was by the Roman culture that largely excluded women from civic and religious functions, the women in the early Celtic churches were recognized as having all the same talents and spiritual authority as men. Stories of the Celtic women saints are particularly fascinating, telling of St. Ita as hearing confessions and forgiving sins, St. Samthann as having a miraculous crozier or staff like that of a bishop, and St. Brigit herself having been ordained. This recognition of women's gifts, of course, was influenced by the ancient Celts, who considered women as being equal to men with similar legal rights, and sharing similar societal roles as tribal leaders, warriors, and spiritual leaders. All of this is alluded to in a ninth-century manuscript, *Catalogue of the Saints in Ireland*, which stated that the early founders of the Celtic Church "did not reject the service and society of women." Many of the women leaders in fact were leaders, like St. Brigit, of monastic communities consisting of both women and men. These "double monasteries" were a normal feature of the earliest monastic life in Ireland and England. (They were also the first to be dissolved when Roman ecclesial authorities gained control over the direction of the Celtic churches.)

Another significant difference that affected the spirituality of Celtic Christians was their closeness to the natural environment. While the Roman church increasingly built its churches in urban areas, sometimes far removed from the forests and lakes, the Celtic Church, mostly rural, built monasteries and hermitages in solitary places, in secluded valleys and forests, on the banks of broad rivers, near cascading streams and ocean tides. These were the locations where nature's inhabitants, animals and birds, would be seen and their melodies heard throughout the day and night, and where natural beauty could be enjoyed. As J. Romilly Allen suggests, "No one who has visited any considerable number of ancient Celtic ecclesiastical buildings can fail to have been struck by the care which the monks took in selecting sites where feeling of religious devotion might be intensified by the contemplation of all that is beautiful in nature." This same sentiment is experienced frequently by those who have visited the valley and lakes of Glendalough, or looked across the River Shannon from its banks at Clonmacnoise; felt the ocean spray after climbing the rock formations at Giant's Causeway, or watched the crashing waves at the Land's Ends in Cornwall, at Saint-Malo in Brittany, and on the coast outside of Santiago de Compostela in Spain.

A story Kenneth Jackson tells of a certain Irish monk by the name of Suibhne Geilt evokes this idyllic world of natural beauty and solitude, surrounded by animals:

> A lovely glen with a lovely green-gushing stream flowing precipitously down over the cliff, and a blessed spot there where there

was a gathering of saints and very many righteous people, and many too were the fair and lovely trees there with heavy luxuriant fruit on that cliff; many also there were the sheltering ivy bushes, and heavy-headed apple trees bending to earth with the weight of their fruit and there were also on that cliff wild deer and hares and great heavy swine, and many too were the fat seals that used to sleep there on that cliff after coming out of the great sea beyond.

Another Irish monk and hermit, Manchán of Liath (d. 665), speaks in his poetry of his deep desire for communion with his natural environment and its inhabitants:

> I wish, O Son of the living God,
> Eternal ancient King,
> For a secret hut in the wilderness
> That it may be my dwelling....
>
> A beautiful wood close by
> Around it on every side
> For the nurture of many-voiced birds
> To shelter and hide it....
>
> This is the housekeeping I would get,
> I would choose it without concealing,
> Fragrant fresh leeks, hens,
> Salmon, trout, bees....
>
> And for me to be sitting for a time
> Praying to God in every place.

Christian Celts had an eye for beauty: the beauty of the body, of the soul, of friendship, of the natural environment.

CELTIC NATURE MYSTICS, POETS, AND SOLITAIRES

This intimacy with nature and deep appreciation of it is beautifully reflected in the early writings of the Christian nature poets, mystics, and hermits of Ireland and Wales who, like the twentieth-century Trappist monk and poet Thomas Merton, loved their hermitages or huts in the wilderness. Hundreds of Irish and Welsh poems have survived—poems that scholars have suggested occupy a unique position in the literature of Western culture, along with the Buddhist and Taoist nature poets of China, Japan, Korea, and other parts of Asia. These Celtic nature poets make constant reference to the presence of animals and birds in their landscapes, and how attuned they were to them, obviously having developed powers of keen observation and attentive listening, considering their frequent references to the animals and birds, and the sounds they made. A virtual Peaceable Kingdom is expressed in one untitled Irish poem, attributed to a certain Deirdre, that could easily be describing the landscape around Glendalough, the monastic site of St. Kevin, situated in an Irish mountain area, surrounded by two lakes:

> Glen of fruits and fish and lakes,
> Peaked hill of lovely wheat....
> Glen full of bees, of the longhorned wild oxen.
>
> Glen of cuckoos and thrushes and blackbirds,
> Precious is its cover to every fox;
> Glen full of wild garlic and watercress and woods,
> Of shamrock and flowers, leafy and twisting-crested.
>
> Sweet are the bellings of the brown-backed dappled deer
> Under the oakwood over the bare hill top,
> Gentle hinds that are timid
> Lying hidden in the great-treed glen.

Introduction

...a slumberous paradise for the badgers
in their quiet burrows with their young....

Glen of the sleek brown round-faced otters
That are pleasant and active in fishing,
Many are the white-winged stately swans,
And salmon breeding along the rocky brink.
...chalk-white starry sunny glen.

In these beautiful, haunting, magical poems, we find mention of "the lonesome cry of the eagle," "the murmur of otters," and "the talk of foxes." We find in them, as we will in the stories of St. Brigit, references to "tame swine, goats, boars, wild swine;" we find "mighty whales," surely like the whale by the name Jasconius in the stories of St. Brendan, patron saint of whales and dolphins. In this nature poetry, we find "hunting dogs and hounds," as we will see in St. Melangell's story; we find reference to deer and "dappled red-breasted fawns," as in the story of St. Patrick saving one; we find allusions to "the music of the wolf pack at the end of the very cold night," as St. Maedoc, a friend of wolves, must have heard in the area where he lived. This nature poetry of Celtic solitaires and mystics makes reference to a crane that "screams over its crags," perhaps like the wearied one that landed on Iona and was saved by St. Columcille; reference to the "brown round-faced otters," which may have looked like those who warmed St. Cuthbert after he spent nights in the cold waters off of Lindisfarne, praying. And, as in St. Kevin's story with the blackbird he protected, we find a blackbird alluded to in another nature poem:

The bird that calls from the willow,
Lovely is its little beak with its clear call,
The melodious yellow bill of the jet-black hardy bird;
A lively tune is sung, the blackbird's note.

Complaints in this Celtic poetry by their writers, yes, of the bitter cold of winters and a longing for spring, of grief and prayers for the dead, "as if every dead person were a special friend," even fear of Viking raids that might destroy their quiet solitude. But overall, overwhelming tones of profound gratitude and great joy.

The hermit's life in this early Celtic Church was one of ascetic simplicity, in imitation of the Desert Christians who had gone into the desert regions of Egypt, Syria, and Palestine, beginning in the third century CE, in search of holiness. Celtic monks loved the stories about these heroic women and men, and they sought to imitate their ascetical lifestyle. For Celtic hermits, in particular, who lived outside the monasteries, it was expected of them to eat and drink only what they found in the surrounding woods or what they could grow in their own gardens. They picked the berries when in season and ate the nuts and the vegetables from the garden. Many seemed to practice a vegetarian diet. One poem describes the landscape around the cell of Marbhan: "An excellent spring, a cup of noble water to drink"; "Acorns, spare berries...a clutch of eggs, honey, produce of wild onions—God has sent it—sweet apples, red whortleberries, crowberries." In the Life of St. Brendan we hear of Barrinthus and his friends coming to an island hermit-monastery where they were greeted lovingly by the brothers who lived there "in harmony in all things": "for no other food or drink was served there but the roots of herbs and the fruits of the trees, and drink of water to sate their thirst." In the Life of St. Kevin of Glendalough, when he had settled there, we are told he lived "without food but nuts of the wood and plants of the ground and pure water to drink." In a commentary on the Life of St. Ciarán of Saighir, we find, "And this was his meal every night, a little barley bread and two roots of murathach and spring water; the skins of wild fawns were his clothing, and damp quilt upon them outside a pillow of stone was what he would sleep upon always."

One of the most remarkable features of the nature poems and the stories of the saints was their very intimate love and sympathy for animals, wild and tame. Irish scholar Kenneth Jackson says that the distinctive thing about the Irish hermit poetry is that, unlike other pastoral traditions, such as the early Greek, who wrote of an appreciation of the natural world, the Irish hermits "lived so much among the wild creatures that they became almost one with them, almost brothers to them, as if they were hardly conscious that there was any distinction of genus." He points out that this is especially clear in the ninth-century poem of the monk and his pet cat, Pangur Ban, which, along with so many other stories in the Lives of the saints, demonstrates this quality of intimacy.

Continual prayer was the hermits' and anchorites' occupation, freedom from distractions and peacefulness was the way of life they desired. In many ways they were doing what the Celts called "soul-making," preparing for a happy death and eternal union with God. Their huts were meant to be places "where spears are not feared," and where they could live "without an hour of quarrel, without the noise of strife," with animals all around them. Robin Flower states that it was the poets' rich spirituality and inner life that made their poetry so powerful. "It was not only that these scribes and anchorites lived by the destiny of their dedication in an environment of wood and sea," he writes; "it was because they brought into that environment an eye washed miraculously clear by a continual spiritual exercise that they, first in Europe, had that strange vision of natural things in an almost unnatural purity." This quality of purity of heart is manifest in a poem by an anonymous hermit:

Over my head the woodland wall
Rises; the ouzel (black bird) sings to me;
Above my booklet lined with words
The woodland birds shake out their glee.

That's the blithe cuckoo chanting clear
In mantle grey from bough to bough!
God keep me still! for here I write
A scripture bright in great woods now.

This is the poetry of the nature mystics in the woods, reflecting a profound appreciation of nature and its inhabitants, expressed too in the stories of the saints, including the Life of St. Declan of Ardmore: "For he was in his own dear cell which he had built, himself for himself. It is between wood and water in a strait and secret spot on the sea's brink, and a clear stream flows by it from the wood to the sea, and trees gird it beautifully round about." Twentieth-century Irish poet and novelist Patrick Kavanagh (1904–67) echoes this same sense of wonder in his book *Tarry Flynn*, whose fictional hero is based upon Kavanagh's own life and mystical beliefs:

> The simple, fantastic beauty of ordinary things growing—
> marsh-marigolds, dandelions, thistles, and grass.

All the Celtic mystics, solitaires, and poets understood the power of poetry, as well as that of stories that are shared.

According to the Irish scholar Kenneth Jackson, about the same time as much of this nature poetry was being written, around the eighth through the tenth centuries, the stories of the Celtic saints were also being transcribed on sheets of vellum and parchment. It is no wonder, considering the ancient stories of the Celtic heroes and deities that preceded those of the saints' and the natural environment in which the Celts lived, that both poetry and saints' stories contain an abundance of references to animals, birds, and, as Kavanagh says, the "fantastic beauty of ordinary things." Repeatedly in the stories of the Celtic saints, we find this kinship with nature and animals: in their awareness that animals are friends, birds have messages, waters can sing, and tree branches have melodies. The ancient Celts' stories of their heroes, passed down orally from generation to generation by bards, was transformed with the arrival of Christianity on their shores into a new form of written literature called *hagiography*. Whether shared around a fire or on the pages of a manuscript or book, both ancient and Christian Celts knew that there was nothing more wonderful than the incomparable, tremendous story. For Christians, nothing was better for teaching wisdom and spirituality than the stories of Jesus and the saints.

STORYTELLERS OF THE CELTIC SAINTS

What some historians call "the golden age" in the Celtic Church is associated with the early Celtic saints who lived primarily in the sixth and seventh centuries, founding their monasteries and spreading Christianity to other lands as well as their own. This age was followed in the late seventh to the thirteenth centuries CE with the writing of their stories in hagiographies or Lives. In the history of Christian spirituality, hagiography is the genre of writing that developed in the early church and is specifically concerned with the lives and holiness of early spiritual leaders in the churches. The term comes from two Greek words *graphe*, which means "writing," and *hagoi*, "about saints." The Christian storytellers who first wrote down the legends of the saints drew upon the rich oral tradition of storytelling about them, which had been kept alive for centuries, preceding any writing. While these stories cannot be considered historical in the strict sense that we understand that term today, they do provide insights into the historical context of the early monastic communities of the Celtic Church and specific values associated with their leaders.

Hagiographers primarily wrote the Lives because they believed that the saint whose life they were describing had something important to teach people about Christian holiness, prayer, service, and union with God. Ultimately, these stories—like those of the gospel stories of Jesus—were written to inspire later generations of Christians in leading a life reflecting the values of their original founder. Although the Gospels themselves do not specifically allude to the presence of animals at Jesus's birth, certainly the nativity narratives of the shepherds visiting him (Luke 2:8–20) and of the wisemen paying homage (Matt 2:1–12) would presume that sheep and possibly camels would have accompanied them. Some apocryphal texts have an ox and donkey worshipping the Christ child, while the earliest artistic depiction of the nativity in a fourth-century sarcophagus from Italy shows him flanked by the ox at his head and the donkey at his feet. Thus, his birth was associated with animals. As an adult, Jesus, in grieving over the fate of Jerusalem, compares himself to a mother hen who wants to gather her chicks to protect them from harm (Matt 23:37–39). In the context of Jesus's life and teachings, it is surely highly significant that the Celtic nature poets and hagiographers portray themselves and the Celtic saints as intimates with animals and birds. In the hagiographies themselves, animals are portrayed as fellow-creatures of the earth who, once befriended, become helpers to the saints, sometimes even assisting them in building their monasteries or acting as spiritual guides.

Although the idea of animals that are helpful and friendly to humans is one that is widely diffused in folklore, in the Lives of the Celtic saints this is abundantly clear. Frequently they are portrayed as protectors of both wild and tame animals, and patrons of them. As the scholar Charles Plummer says,

> Often does the saint interpose to save a hunted animal from its pursuers, or renders fierce animals tame, or feeds starving wolves out of the herds which he tends....Often the saint's place of set-tlement is fixed by the appearance of animals, whether foretold beforehand, or accepted on the spot as an omen. His burial place is determined in the same way. It is clear that the ideas underlying many of these stories go back to a time when no hard and fast line was drawn between men and animals, when it seemed quite natural that the language of animals should be understood by men and vice versa, that an animal should have human under-standing and enter into a man's thoughts; that covenants should be made with them.

Those who later wrote about the early Celtic saints, including Bede the Venerable, "were really lovers of animals" and their saints "shared this qual-ity to the full."

In that light, we will discover in the following stories that both saints *and animals* are to be seen as soul friends and mediators of wisdom, capable of inspiring a deeper spirituality, a new ethic of holiness for our own time. Let us turn now to those stories, allowing them to become our spiritual mentors and guides. As we reflect upon these tales, let us ask the question of what each story has to teach us about our own spirituality and call to service and leadership today. What lessons or virtues is the story affirming for our own lives? These stories reveal a profound kinship of the saints with animals, and animals with the saints. What are they teaching us about wisdom and a spirituality that might well change our lives and our attitudes toward all of creation and the loving God who made us all? As St. Columban said so wisely many centuries ago, "If you wish to know the Creator, come to know his creatures."

Stories of the Celtic Saints

THE HOLY TRINITY OF
CELTIC SAINTS

1N THE STORIES OF PATRICK, BRIGIT, AND COLUMCILLE, "the Holy Trinity of Celtic Saints," we find numerous examples of the saints' loving treatment of animals.

PATRICK OF ARMAGH

PERHAPS THE MOST WELL-KNOWN Celtic saint of all times is Patrick, who lived from about 390 to 461 CE. The patron saint of Ireland, he was, however, not born there, but possibly near the west coast of England or Wales or, more likely, Brittany. Raised in a Christian family (his father was a deacon and his grandfather a priest), Patrick, at the age of fifteen, was captured by Irish pirates and taken against his will to Ireland where he lived for six years as a slave. There, while tending sheep, alone on a mountainside except most likely accompanied by a dog (a great variety of dogs, from wolfhounds to greyhounds to terriers, lapdogs, and collies, were common then), he experienced a religious conversion. As he writes in an autobiography, *The Confession*, about his experience shepherding "day after day," "More and more the love of God grew strong within me." Visited by voices and dreams, he escaped back to his homeland after six years, only to return to Ireland following another vivid dream in which he heard the voices of the Irish: "Come back, O youth, and walk among us once more." The earliest hagiography of Patrick, by Muirchu, written some two hundred years after the saint's death, contains stories relating how Patrick changes himself and his men into deer in order to hide from a pursuing chieftain who refused to accept the new Christian faith the saint was preaching. Another deer story tells how on the hilltop near Armagh, Ireland, where a church still stands today, he comes upon a hind (a female deer) with her fawn while searching for a place to build his monastery.

Patrick's feast day, of course, as everyone knows, is March 17.

Patrick's Shape-shifting

When Patrick had returned to Ireland to bring the Irish the gospel, a certain King Loegaire, with his followers who had not converted, was angry with Patrick, and he determined to kill him. Loegaire said to his men, "Lay hands on this fellow who is destroying us." At this, Patrick rose and said in a clear voice, "May God arise and his enemies be scattered and those who hate him flee from his face." And immediately darkness fell on them, and there was a horrible sort of upheaval and the ungodly attacked one another. There was a great earthquake that locked their chariot-axles together and drove them off violently, until in the end only a few of them escaped half-dead to the mountain Monduirn. The king was left with only seven men; himself and his wife and two kings and another four followers. And they were very frightened. The queen came to Patrick and said to him, "Sir, you are just and powerful; do not destroy the king, for the king will come and bend the knee before you, and worship your Lord." The king came, then, compelled by fear, and bowed before the saint and pretended to worship the God whom he did not want to accept. After they had taken leave of each other, the king, going a little way off, called St. Patrick over on some pretext, with the intention of killing him. But Patrick, aware of the wicked king's thoughts, first blessed his companions in the name of Jesus Christ, and turned toward the king. The king counted them as they approached, and immediately they disappeared from the king's sight—he and his men only saw eight deer with a fawn heading, as it were, for the wilds. King Loegaire, saddened, frightened, and humiliated, returned at dawn to Tara with the few survivors. Patrick, following the Lord Jesus's command to go forth and teach all nations and baptize them in the name of the Father and of the Son and of the Holy Spirit, set out from Tara and preached, with the Lord working with him and confirming his words with powerful signs.

Patrick and His Charioteer's Horses

One night, as Patrick and his men moved across Ireland in their attempt to convert more people to Christianity, his charioteer realized that his horses had gone astray and was grieving about this as if he had just lost close friends. He told Patrick, but as it was dark, he could not go and search for them. Patrick was moved to kindness like a godly father, and said to the tearful charioteer, "God is always ready to help us in our difficulties, and he grants us his mercy in all our misfortunes. So you shall find these horses that you are crying over." Then, holding out his hand and drawing clear his sleeve, Patrick raised his hand and his five fingers shone out like spotlights. They lit up all the area around about them and in that light the man was able to find his missing horses, and to stop crying. But it should be noted that this miracle was not known about during Patrick's lifetime because the charioteer told no one about it until after Patrick's death.

Patrick Saves a Fawn

Sometime later, there was in the country a rich and respected man called Daire. Patrick asked him to give him some place for his religious observances. And the rich man said to the saint, "What place do you want?" Patrick said, "I want you to give me that piece of high ground which is called Willow Ridge, and I will build a monastery there." And they both went out, St. Patrick and Daire, to look at the wonderful offering and pleasing gift, and they climbed up to that high ground and found a hind with her little fawn lying on the spot where now there is the altar of the north church in Armagh. Patrick's companions, however, wanted to take hold of the fawn and kill it, but the saint refused and did not allow it;

indeed the saint himself took the fawn, carrying it on his shoulders, and the hind followed him like a very gentle, docile ewe, until he had let the fawn go free in another wood lying to the north side of Armagh, where the knowledgeable say there are some signs remaining to this day of his miraculous power.

BRIGIT OF KILDARE

BRIGIT LIVED IN IRELAND from about 452 to 524 CE, governing both women and men in her double monastery at Kildare. She seems to have had all the powers of a bishop in her community, and there are even stories of her having been ordained as such by a Bishop Mel. Considered one of the "holy trinity" of Irish saints—Patrick and Columcille being the other two—she has so many stories of her great compassion for both humans and animals that she is similar to the bodhisattva Quan Yin, the Buddhist goddess of mercy, who is worshipped in China, Japan, and other East Asian countries, and who is, like Brigit, seen as the protector of animals. In Ireland, Brigit is still prayed to as the guardian of farm animals. Her Life was written by Cogitosus, a monk at Kildare, in about 650 CE. In the stories about her, she is portrayed as an exceptionally kind person to both her fellow-humans, especially the poor and lepers, as well as animals of every kind, all of whom seem to have responded to her love with trust and gratitude.

Brigit's feast day is February 1.

Brigit and the Hungry Dog

As Brigit grew into adulthood, everything to which her hand was set used to increase. She tended sheep, she satisfied the birds, she fed the poor. Once when a noble guest came to her father Dubthach's house, hospitality was naturally expected to be shown. Five pieces of bacon were given to Brigit to be boiled. A hungry hound came into the house, however, and to the kitchen where Brigit was cooking. Out of pity for him Brigit gave him the fifth piece of bacon. The hound, however, was not satisfied with that. So Brigit gave him another piece. She thought that the guest was asleep, and would not see this, but he did and went to Dubthach to complain. Dubthach then unhappily asked his daughter, "Have you boiled the bacon, and do all the portions remain?" "Count them," Brigit responded, and when her father counted them he discovered that not one of them was missing! This was a relief to him, but he was not happy about the guest's accusation, and as a result, the guest was not given the bacon. At Brigit's suggestion, it was given to the poor and needy, while the happy hound went away filled as well.

The Wild Fox and Brigit's Compassion

On a certain occasion, when a foolish man saw a fox walking toward the castle of the Irish king, he thought it was a wild animal. Dimwitted as he was, he was ignorant of the fact that the fox was tame, a frequent visitor to the king's court trained in various skills. It was, in short, a grand and distinguished mascot of the king and his nobles. While a huge crowd watched, the poor fool killed the fox. At once, the man was denounced by those who had witnessed the deed, put in irons, and dragged before the king. When the king learned what had happened, he was enraged. He ordered the man to be killed, unless a fox, as clever as his own, were given to him in recompense. The king also ordered that the man's wife, his children, and all his family be reduced to slavery.

When holy and venerable Brigit learned what had happened, she felt great compassion for the miserable fool and ordered her chariot to be prepared. Grieving in her innermost heart for the poor unfortunate who was unjustly condemned, she rode along the road that led to the castle of the king, pouring out prayers to God as she passed over the flat plain. There was no delay, for the Lord heard Brigit as she continued to pray so fervently. He commanded one of his foxes to go to her. When the fox approached the speeding chariot of holy Brigit, it leaped up lightly and landed inside. Then nestling up under the fold of Brigit's garment, it sat tamely in the chariot with her. As Brigit arrived at the king's castle, she began to beg that the poor fool who was being held be set free. The king was unwilling to listen to her pleas, swearing that he would not free the man unless he were recompensed with a fox as gentle and as clever as his had been.

At this point Brigit brought forth her fox into the center of the court. The fox played before the eyes of everyone in exactly the same way as the other fox had done, acting before the king and all those gathered there with the same gestures, cleverness, and docility as the first. When the king saw this, he was satisfied, and acknowledging the resounding approval of the multitude who were in admiration of this wondrous event, he ordered the man who had earlier been charged with the crime to be released and set free. Not much later, when St. Brigit had returned to her home, the same fox, sad and tormented by the crowds, fled quickly through the remote forests and reached its own cave unharmed.

The Wide Variety of Animals Who Listened to Brigit and Loved Her

On one occasion, a single wild boar, which was being hunted, came running out of the woods in terror and suddenly landed amid blessed Brigit's pigs. She noted its arrival and pronounced a blessing upon it; thereupon the boar lost its terror and settled down among the herd. See, brothers and sisters, how even brute animals and creatures were unable to resist her words and her will but served her tamely and obediently. On another day, the blessed Brigit saw some ducks swimming on the water, occasionally taking wing. Being moved with affection for them, she commanded them to come to her. A great flock of them flew over to her on feathered wings with eager obedience to her words and showing no fear, as if they were used to people. She touched them with her hands and caressed them for a while, before they returned to their place of origin. From so many other stories we can easily conclude that all kinds of wild animals, flocks, and birds listened to her and loved her.

COLUMCILLE OF IONA

THE THIRD SAINT OF "the holy trinity," Columcille lived from 521–97 CE. He was born in Donegal, Ireland, and after his ordination as a priest, founded numerous monasteries in Ireland, including Derry, Durrow, and Kells. All of these had oak groves, the favorite trees of druids and druidesses, growing on their original sites. (Kildare, for example, the site of St. Brigit's monastery, where originally an "eternal flame" was kept burning by druidesses, means "church of the oak.") At the age of forty-two, Columcille left Ireland and moved to the island of Iona in 563 CE where he founded one of the greatest monasteries in the early Celtic Church, still a very popular place of pilgrimage today. A poet, scholar, and writer, he too has stories, written about him by Adamnan (c. 624–704), the ninth abbot of that monastery, expressing his care for animals and birds, and their love for him in return. The most famous, perhaps, is the one of his solicitude for a tired crane, revealing that, as much as the Rule of St. Benedict encourages every guest to be treated as another Christ (chap. 53), here in Columcille's monastery evidently even animals should be treated in that way! Another, less known, included here is one that suggests that his compassion was manifest in his demand that no animals be killed or eaten at his monastery, suggesting that he was a vegetarian, if not outright vegan. (Other saints, as we will see, followed a similar diet.) Such love and compassion toward animals, it seems, was well-received, for in another story, as Columcille prepares to die, a wonderful, but grieving white horse comes to tell him goodbye.

Columcille's feast day is June 9.

Columcille and the Tired Crane

While Columcille was living on Iona, he called one of the brothers to him and said,

Three days from now, in the morning, you must sit down and wait for a crane on the shore on the western side of this island. A stranger from the northern region of Ireland, it has been driven about by various winds. This crane will come, weary and fatigued, after the ninth hour (3:00 p.m.). It will lie down before you on the beach quite exhausted. Treat that bird tenderly, and take it to some nearby house, where you can kindly and carefully nurse it and feed it for three days and three nights. When the crane is refreshed after three days of rest, and is no longer willing to stay with us, it will fly back with renewed strength to the pleasant part of Ireland from which it originally came. I entrust this bird to you with special care because it comes from our native land.

The brother obeyed Columcille, and on the third day, after the ninth hour, he watched as he had been told for the arrival of the expected guest. As soon as the crane came and alighted on the shore, he gently picked up the weak and hungry bird and carried it to a dwelling that was nearby, where he fed it. On the monk's return to the monastery that evening, Columcille, without any inquiry, but as if stating a fact, said to him, "God bless you, my son, for your kind attention to this foreign visitor which will not remain here for very long, but will return within three days to its old home." It happened exactly as the saint predicted, for after being nursed carefully for three days, the bird flapped its wings and gently rose to great height in the sight of its hospitable host. Then, on that calm day, it made its way through the air homeward, flying straight across the sea to Ireland.

Columcille's Admonition to Do No Harm

Another time, a certain brother called Molua approached the saint while he was writing, and said, "Please bless this implement that I am holding." Stretching out his holy hand a little, with the pen still in it, he made the sign of the cross over it without looking up from the book that he was copying. Now when Molua had gone away with the blessed implement, Columcille said as an afterthought, "What was that implement that

I blessed for our brother?" "A knife," said Diarmait, his faithful attendant, "for slaughtering bulls and cattle." "I trust in my Lord," the saint replied, "that the implement I blessed will do no harm to people or animals." These words of Columcille came true that very hour. For the same brother went out beyond the enclosure of the monastery intending to kill a bullock. Three times he tried, pressing hard, but he could not pierce the skin. So the skillful monks melted down the iron knife and coated all the implements of the monastery with it, and after that none of these could do any harm, since the saint's blessing remained on them so strongly.

Columcille and the White Horse

As a true prophet, Columcille knew long before his death when he would die. One day during the month of May, the old man, worn out with age, went in a chariot to visit some of the brethren who were at work. When he had found them on the western side of Iona, he began to speak to them, saying, "With great yearning, during the paschal solemnities this past April, I desired to depart to Christ the Lord, and he gave me permission to do so, if I wished. But rather than have a joyous feast turned for you into mourning, I thought it better to put off for a little longer the time of my departure from the world." All the while the beloved monks were hearing this sad news, they were greatly affected, and he tried as best as he could to cheer them with words of consolation. Then, having done this, he turned his face to the east, still seated as he was in his chariot, and blessed the island with its inhabitants. From that day to the present, the venomous reptiles with the three forked tongues could do no harm to man nor beast.

Halfway back to the monastery, he rested at a place where a cross was later erected. It is standing to this day, fixed into a millstone, and can be observed on the roadside. While the saint, bowed down with old age, sat there to rest a little, a white packhorse came up to him. It was the same willing servant that used to carry the milk vessels from the cowshed to the monastery. As it came up to the saint, it laid its head on his bosom—inspired by God to do so, I believe, since each animal is gifted with the knowledge of things according to the will of the Creator. Somehow knowing that its master was soon about to leave it, and that it would see him no more, this white horse began to neigh plaintively, and like a human being, to shed copious tears on the saint's chest. When his attendant saw this, he began to drive the weeping mourner away, but the saint forbade him, saying, "Let it be, Diarmait. Since it is so fond of me, let it shed its tears of grief on my chest. Consider this: since you are human and have a rational soul, you cannot know anything of my departure, except what I myself have just told you. But to this humble beast, devoid of reason, the Creator Himself has evidently in some way revealed that its master is about to leave it." Saying this, the saint blessed the horse, which sadly turned away from him.

AND THE OTHERS

BRENDAN OF CLONFERT

PROBABLY THE MOST WELL-KNOWN Celtic saint, after the holy trinity of saints, is Brendan the Navigator, whose journey, *Voyage of Brendan*, became one of the most popular stories of the Middle Ages. Written possibly as early as 800 CE in Ireland, it tells of his search for the Promised Land of the Saints, and became so popular that it influenced a number of explorers, including Christopher Columbus, to set sail into the unknown from Europe. The epic of Brendan's voyage is an example of that literary genre, peculiar to Ireland, called an *immram*, associated with the seafaring adventures of Celtic heroes. Brendan's story seems to have been influenced by an immram tale of a pre-Christian adventurer, the *Voyage of Bran*, and influential in another immram story, the *Voyage of Mael Duin*. Some of the adventures described in Brendan's also seem to have been influenced by Homer's *Odyssey* and Virgil's *Aeneid*, which Irish monks would have known about at the time Brendan's voyage was written down. Some believe that his story is actually an account of his travel to Greenland, if not North America itself. Brendan, the saint, though his life is associated with fabulous legends and adventures, was a real person who lived from 486 to 578 CE. He was born on the west coast of Ireland, founded a number of monasteries, the most famous that of Clonfert about 559, and did make voyages to the Scottish isles and perhaps to Wales and northwestern England as well. The *Voyage of Brendan* is filled with stories of animals, from a helpful dog, and birds who guide him and his monks, to a whale who provides shelter, and to references about Brendan's own decision to never eat meat.

Brendan is considered the patron saint of boatmen, mariners, travelers, elderly adventurers, and whales. His feast day is May 16.

Brendan and His Monks Set Sail, Helped by a Dog Who Guides Them

St. Brendan and those with him got iron tools and constructed a light boat ribbed with wood and with a wooden frame, as is usual in those parts. They covered it with ox-hides tanned with the bark of oak and smeared all the joints of the hides on the outside with fat. They carried into the boat hides for the makings of two other boats, supplies for forty days, fat for preparing hides to cover the boat, and other things needed for human life. They also placed a mast in the middle of the boat and a sail and the other requirements for steering a boat. Then St. Brendan ordered his brothers in the name of the Father, Son, and Holy Spirit to enter the boat. St. Brendan then embarked, the sail was spread, and they began to steer westward into the summer solstice. They had a favorable wind and, apart from holding the sail, had no need to navigate. After fifteen days the wind dropped. They set themselves to the oars until their strength failed. St. Brendan quickly began to comfort and advise them, saying, "Brothers, do not fear. God is our helper, sailor, and helmsman, and he guides us. Ship all the oars and the rudder. Just leave the sail spread and God will do as he wishes with his servants and their ship."

They always had their food, however, at evening time. When they got a wind, they did not know from what direction it came or in what direction the boat was going. When forty days were up and all the victuals had been consumed, an island appeared to them toward the north, rocky and high. When they had circled the island for three days, on the third day about three o'clock they found an opening where one boat might enter. St. Brendan stood up immediately and blessed the entry. It was a cutting with rock of remarkable height on either side, straight up like a wall. When they had all disembarked and stood outside on land, St. Brendan forbade them to take any equipment out of the boat. As they were walking along the cliffs of the sea, a dog ran across them on a path and came to the feet of St. Brendan as dogs usually come to heel to their master. St. Brendan said to his brothers, "Has not God sent us a good messenger? Follow him." Then St. Brendan and his brothers followed the dog to a town. On entering the town, they caught sight of a great hall, furnished with beds and chairs, and water for washing their tired feet. After entering, St. Brendan spoke to a man, "Bring the meal that God has sent us." This man found a table, made it ready for them, and brought each of them a loaf of marvelous whiteness and some fish. When all were brought before him, St. Brendan blessed the meal and said to his brothers, "Give praise to the God of heaven who gives food to all flesh."

Brendan and the Whale

One day as Brendan and his fellow-monks were traversing the sea in search of the Promised Land, they approached an island that had no grass growing on it. There were a few pieces of driftwood on it, but no sand on its shore. Disembarking on it, the brothers spent the night outside in prayers and vigils while Brendan remained sitting inside the boat. He knew what kind of island it was, but did not want to tell them, lest they be terrified. When morning came, while Brendan sang the Mass in the boat, some of the brothers put a pot over a fire they had started in order to cook the raw meat. Suddenly, however, when the wood was burning and the pot began to boil, the island began to heave and sway like a wave hitting a shore. The brothers rushed to the boat, crying out for protection to the holy man. Clasping their hands, Brendan drew each one of them into the boat. Once everyone was onboard, they quickly left the island and set sail. Then, before their bewildered eyes, the island itself on which they had camped moved out to sea! Their lighted fire could be seen over two miles away. It was only then that Brendan told the brothers what it really was, saying, "Brothers, are you surprised at what this island has done?" They responded in unison, "Dear Father, not only are we surprised, but, truly, we are terrified." He, in response, gently told them, "My sons, don't be afraid. God revealed to me during the night in a dream the secret of this happening. Where we were was not an island, but a fish—and no ordinary fish, but a whale, the most giant fish that swims in the ocean. His name is Jasconius. Do not be afraid; he will offer us a place for shelter again." And then, smiling broadly, he also advised, "Just don't light any more fires on his back!"

The Paradise of Birds, and the One Who Offers Hope and Guidance

When they were sailing near the island where they had spent the three days, and came to the western edge of it, they saw another island almost joining it, separated only by a small channel. There was plenty of grass on it; it had groves of trees and was full of flowers. They started circling it, looking for a landing place. As they were sailing on its southern side, they found a stream flowing into the sea, and there they put the boat in to land. As they disembarked, St. Brendan ordered them to draw the boat with ropes up along the riverbed with all their might. The father sat in the boat. So they carried on for about a mile, until they came to the source of the stream. St. Brendan spoke, "Our Lord Jesus Christ has given us a place in which to stay during his holy resurrection." And he added, "If we had no other supplies but this spring, it would, I believe, alone be enough for food and drink." Over the spring there was a tree of extraordinary girth and no less height covered with white birds. They covered it so much that one could scarcely see its leaves or branches. When the man of God saw this, he began to think and ponder within himself what it meant or what was the reason that such a great multitude of birds could be all collected together. He was so tormented about this that the tears poured out and flowed down upon his cheeks, and he implored God, saying, "God, who knows the unknown and reveals all that is secret, you know the distress of my heart. I implore your majesty to have pity and reveal to me, a sinner, through your great mercy your secret that I now look upon with my eyes. I rely not on what I deserve or my worth, but rather on your boundless pity."

When he said this within himself and had taken his seat again, one of the birds flew from the tree, making a noise with her wings like a handbell, and took up position on the side of the boat where the man of God was sitting. She sat on the edge of the prow and stretched her wings, as it were as a sign of joy, and looked with a peaceful mien at the holy father. The man of God immediately concluded that God had listened to his plea, and spoke to the bird, "If you are God's messenger, tell me where these birds come from or for what reason they are congregated here." She replied immediately,

> We survive from the great destruction of the ancient enemy, but we were not associated with them through any sin of ours. When we were created, Lucifer's fall and that of his followers brought about our destruction also. But our God is just and true. In his great judgment he sent us here. We endure no sufferings. Here we can see God's presence. But God has separated us from sharing the lot of the others who were faithful. We wander through various regions of the air and the firmament and the earth, just like the other spirits that travel on their missions. But on holy days and Sundays we are given bodies such as you now see so that we may stay here and praise our Creator. You and your brothers have now spent one year on your journey. Six still remain. Where you celebrated Easter today, there you will celebrate it every year. Afterwards you will find what you cherish in your heart, that is, the Promised Land of the Saints.

When she said this, she lifted herself off the prow and flew to the other birds.

Brendan, Vegetarian or Vegan

The venerable father and his companions sailed out into the ocean, and their boat was carried along for forty days. One day there appeared to them a beast of immense size following them at a distance. He spouted foam from his nostrils and ploughed through the waves at a great speed, as if he were about to devour them. St. Brendan comforted his companions, saying, "Do not be afraid. You have little faith. God, who always defends us, though, will deliver us from the mouth of this beast and from other dangers." As the beast came near them, he caused waves of extraordinary height to go before him right up to the boat, so that the brothers were more and more afraid. The venerable elder raised his hands to heaven and said, "Lord, deliver your servants, as you delivered David from the hand of Goliath, the giant. Lord, deliver us, as you delivered Jonas from the belly of the whale." After these pleas asking for deliverance, a mighty monster passed near them from the west going to encounter the beast. This monster immediately attacked him, emitting fire from his mouth. The wretched beast that pursued the servants of Christ was cut into three pieces before their eyes. The other returned to where he had come from.

The next day they saw at a distance a very large island full of trees. While they were drawing near its shore and disembarking from the boat, they saw the end portion of the beast that had been slain. St. Brendan said, "See what wished to devour you, you shall now devour! Take your provisions from that beast, enough for three months. For tonight its flesh will be devoured by other beasts." The brothers set out to the place to do so. They brought back as much as they could carry. The venerable father said to them, "Keep it and preserve it carefully with salt. You will have need of it. For God will make the weather fine today, tomorrow, and after tomorrow. The swell of the sea and the waves will fall. Then we will leave this place." When these days were over St. Brendan ordered his brothers to load the boat, to fill the containers and other vessels, and collect plants and roots for his own use. For the father from the time of his ordination to the priesthood tasted nothing in which the spirit of life drew support from flesh. When all was loaded into the boat, they raised the sail and set off in a northerly direction, toward the promised land of the Saints.

CIARAN OF SAIGHIR

CIARAN IS CONSIDERED THE FIRST saint to have been born in Ireland, about 446 CE, and died about 530. One of St. Patrick's earliest disciples, he is said to have received his early education in Tours in Gaul and Rome, where he was ordained. He then went to live as a hermit near Saighir, told to do so by Patrick himself. There, near the Slieve Bloom Mountains, in a solitary forest on the bank of a small stream, he built a hut of wattles and twigs, smeared with mud and thatched with leaves and grass. A vegetarian, he ate only a little barley bread and herbs, and his drink was water from the well. Although many disciples joined him, attracted by his holiness, his first monks, as we discover in the stories about him, were wild animals in the forest.

Ciaran's feast day is March 5.

Ciaran's First Miracle: Saving a Small Bird

The most blessed Ciaran, the first-begotten of the Saints of Ireland, belonged to the west border of Leinster, which is called Ossory. At the time of his birth, none of the folk of Ireland were Christian. His father was called Luaigne, his mother Liadain. Ciaran was brought up on Cape Clear Island. Truly God chose him from his mother's womb, for when the name of Christ was not yet heard in Ireland, the strength of the Christian faith began to grow in him. His parents wondered at this, and all who saw him, at the soberness of his mind, the gentleness of his nature, the sweetness of his words, his timely fasting, his wise counsels, and the other qualities that belong to holy people. One day on this same Cape Clear Island, the first of St. Ciaran's miracles occurred. For when he was still a lad, a hawk swept down from the sky upon a small bird sitting on its nest, caught it before Ciaran's eyes, and carried it off in its talons into the air. The youth saw it, was in deep grief over it, and prayed for the poor captive. Immediately the eagle flew down with its prey, and laid the small bird, mangled and half-dead, before him. Under the pitying gaze of the lad, the poor creature by God's grace was made whole, to his heart's desire, and before his eyes sat brooding on its nest, happy and unhurt.

Ciaran's First Monks:
Brothers Fox, Badger, Wolf, and Deer

For thirty years, Ciaran lived in Ireland, in holiness and integrity of body and soul, without baptism, for the Irish had not been converted to Christianity. Nevertheless, by the inspiration of the Holy Spirit, Ciaran lived devout and perfect in his ways. Hearing a report of the Christian faith in the city of Rome, he left Ireland, and set out for Rome. On reaching it, he was baptized and taught the Christian faith. There he remained for twenty years, reading the Holy Scriptures, and collecting books on their meaning. Seeing the wisdom, devotion, and faith of Ciaran, the Roman people ordained him bishop, and then sent him back to Ireland, his own land. On the road back through Italy, Ciaran met St. Patrick, and the two saints, in meeting face-to-face, were extremely happy. And Patrick said to Ciaran, "Go to Ireland before me; and make your way to a well in the heart of Ireland, on the border between the men of the North and the men of the South. The well is called Fuaran, the little cold well, and there found your monastery, for in that place shall your glory and your resurrection be." The two servants of God kissed and blessed each other, and St. Ciaran went on his way toward Ireland, but the blessed Patrick stayed behind in Italy.

Now when Ciaran arrived in Ireland, God guided him to the well of Fuaran. The blessed Ciaran began to live as a hermit there, for the place was a vast solitude and thick with forest. And he built himself a poor cell that became the beginning of a monastery. And thereafter by God's gift, and through the grace of Ciaran, a city grew up. Now when St. Ciaran first came to that place, he sat himself down under a tree, and under the shadow of it was a fierce boar. The boar, seeing for the first time the face of a human, fled in terror. But then, made tame by God, he came back to Ciaran volunteering to be his servant. That boar was St. Ciaran's first disciple or monk, as one might say, in that place. Immediately the boar, as the man of God watched, began with great vigor to tear down twigs and grass with his teeth to build him a little hut. At that time there was no one with the saint, for he had left his disciples behind when he escaped alone to the solitary place. Later on, other animals came from their dens in the wilds to St. Ciaran, a fox, a badger, a wolf, and a deer, and they stayed with him, tame and gentle. And they obeyed the saint's words in all things, as if they had been his monks.

The Wily Fox and Assertive Badger

One day the Fox, who was shrewder and wilier than the other animals, stole his abbot's shoes, and abandoning his vow of poverty, carried them off to his ancient dwelling in the forest where he intended to chew them. Knowing this, Ciaran sent another monk, namely the Badger, into the forest after the Fox, to bring back his brother to the monastery. So the Badger, being well acquainted with the woods, at once set out in obedience to his abbot's orders, and made his way to the den of Brother Fox. There, finding him about to gnaw his master's slippers, he bit his ears and his tail, cropped his fur, and forced him to return with him to the monastery, there to do penance for his theft. The Fox, driven by necessity, and the Badger with him, carrying the shoes none the worse, came to Ciaran in his cell. The saint said to the Fox, "Why, brother, did you do this evil deed, which good monks would not do? Behold, our water is sweet and free to us, and food is here for us all alike to share. And if you had a longing, as is your nature, to eat flesh, Almighty God would have made it for you from the roots of these trees, if we had asked him." The Fox begged the saint's forgiveness, and did penance, fasting, not eating until he was given the saint's okay. And thereafter he lived sociably with the others.

In the end, Ciaran's disciples and many others sought him out from all parts of Ireland, and it was the beginning of a famous monastery. The animals, however, continued to live there as well, for the rest of their lives, tame and loyal, for the saint was happy to see them as friends and fellow-monks.

COLMAN OF KILMACDUAGH

There are over fifty recognized saints with the name of Colman in Ireland, but the one who is associated with the wonderful story of his animal friends was Colman mac Duagh, who was born in Kiltartan, now County Galway, and lived from about 560 to 632 CE. He was the son of Queen Rhinagh and her husband, the chieftain named Duac, and thus, in Irish, was known as mac Duagh. Educated at St. Enda's monastery on Inishmore, the largest of the Aran Islands, he lived as a hermit there, praying and fasting constantly. Seeking greater solitude, he moved to the Burren in County Claire around 590, accompanied by a servant, where he lived in a cave. Later, with his relative, an Irish king, he founded the monastery of Kilmacduagh ("the church of the son of Duac") in 610, where he was abbot for years. The ruins of this monastery, consisting of seven churches and a large, leaning round tower, are located near the town of Gort in County Galway, a holy site visited by numerous pilgrims today. Among Colman's relics, his crozier can now be seen in the National Museum in Dublin.

Colman's feast day is October 29.

Colman's Friends: The Rooster, the Mouse, and the Fly

Now, among all the other virtues that the Holy Spirit had endowed Colman, he was a great lover of poverty, and kept no earthly possessions, nor gifts, nor any property of his own—unless you could call three small creatures property. For Colman did have three creatures, a rooster, a mouse, and a fly, which he considered to be friends of his. And each served him out of their love for him. Like an alarm clock, the rooster awakened him at a certain time of night with its crowing so that he might not miss the communal prayers at that hour. The service of the other two creatures was even more remarkable. The mouse would not allow the man of God to sleep nor lie at peace beyond the fixed hour that Colman had fixed for himself in his holy vows. When his body and his tired limbs were worn out with vigil and prayer and his other austerities, when his body craved sleep and rest beyond what he had vowed, the mouse, sometimes gnawing at his clothes, sometimes by nibbling at his ear, would drag him from all quiet. Colman was grateful for this service, for he helped him maintain his own self-respect so that his vows were kept.

Scarcely less remarkable was the service of the fly. For when the man of God had leisure to read his holy books, the fly would trot up and down the lines, acting as a living reading aid. If someone would call Colman or he had to do some monastic task, he would instruct the fly to sit down upon the line at which he had stopped reading and keep his place until he could return to finish. The fly always would happily do so for his friend. Marvelous were these small creatures, contributing to the well-being of the monk. Truly they were manifestations of God's grace in his life, and of Christ's gift to the saints. For this, Colman was exceptionally grateful to the God who created all of them, and to his friends, the rooster, the mouse, and the fly, for their services to him that made his daily life so blessed.

COLUMBAN OF LUXEUIL

COLUMBAN IS CONSIDERED the greatest of Ireland's many missionaries to the European continent in the early middle ages. In more recent times, he has been described, because of his knowledge of literature, composition of poetry, and his exquisite writing, as "Ireland's first man of letters," and, because of his prescient sense of European unity, as "Ireland's first European," and a "father of Christian Europe." He was born in Leinster, Ireland, about 543 CE, probably of a noble family who was able to provide him with a good classical education before he became a monk. St. Comgall was an important mentor for him when he joined the seaside monastery at Bangor on the Irish coast, where he was educated, ordained, and lived for many years. In 590, at midlife, Columban, accompanied by twelve companions, including St. Gall, left for Brittany and Gaul to spread the gospel. When he arrived in Gaul, he began a monastery at Annegray. As more followers joined him, he founded another at Luxeuil, and still another near some springs at Fontes (now called Fontaine). Columban and Gall eventually moved on to Switzerland where Gall remained, while the older man settled near Bobbio, Italy, dying in 615. His beautiful white marble tomb can still be seen there. St. Francis of Assisi was one of the more famous pilgrims who visited it, and several nature and animal stories later associated with Francis were originally found in Columban's hagiography, written by Jonas, a monk of Bobbio. The following stories show how much Columban loved and respected animals, and they, in turn, him.

Columban's feast day is November 23.

Columban's Search for Solitude and His Encounters with Bears

When Columban arrived in Gaul, he and his followers settled in an isolated place, called from ancient times Anagrates (Annegray). Despite the loneliness, wilderness, and rocks, they settled there. Then crowds of people and throngs of the infirm, seeking aid in all their sicknesses, began to crowd about Columban in order that he might restore their health. Unable to ignore their pleas, he healed the infirmities of all who came to him through his prayers and by relying upon the help of God. Later, Columban withdrew from his cell, desiring to go deeper into solitude. He entered the wilderness by a longer road and found an immense cliff with steep sides and rocky paths. Perceiving a hollow in the rock, he entered a cave and began to explore its hidden recesses, only to discover that it was the home of a bear—and that the bear herself was there! Columban ordered the beast to leave and to not return to that place. Mercifully, the bear left immediately and did not return. This place was about seven miles from Annegray.

It became Columban's custom to separate himself from the company of others and to dwell in solitary places so that when the feasts of the Lord or saints' days came, he might, with his mind wholly free from disquieting cares, devote himself to prayer. One time, Columban, a lover of solitude, happened to be walking through a dense forest of fruit trees and found a bear about to devour the body of a stag that wolves had killed. The man of God approached the bear, which was licking up the stag's blood, but before it had eaten any of its flesh, he ordered it not to injure the hide that the saint needed for shoes. Then the beast, contrary to its nature, put aside its ferocity, became gentle, and without a murmur, left the stag. The man of God returned to the brethren and told them of his encounter and ordered them to go and strip the hide from the body of the stag.

The Friendly Wolves

Another time while the saint was walking in the dark woods, a book on his shoulder, and arguing with himself about Holy Scripture, the thought came suddenly to his mind whether he would rather choose to suffer the outrage of men, or the savagery of beasts. His thought drove him hard, and he would often cross himself and pray. Finally, he said to himself that it was better to suffer the ferocity of wild beasts that was no sin of theirs, than the cruelty of men, to the loss of their own souls. As he turned this over in his mind, he saw twelve wolves come toward him, and stand about him on the right and on the left, himself in the middle of them. He stood motionless, saying, "God, look to my help; Lord, make haste to help me." They came nearer, and their muzzles touched his clothes! While he stood unshaken, they turned and left him there unterrified, and on to their roaming through the woods.

Columban's Peaceable Kingdom

Marvel not that bird and beast should obey the command of the man of God. For a servant and disciple of Columban saw evidence of the holy man's intimacy with animals. This servant by the name of Chamnoald, who later became a bishop at Lyons, used to tell that he often saw Columban when he was walking in the forest to fast and to pray, and how the holy man would call the creatures of the wild, birds and beasts, to him, and how they would come at once. He would stroke them with his hand and caress them; and the wild things and the birds would leap and skip about him for sheer happiness, jumping up on him as puppies jump on their masters. Even that small wild creature, the squirrel, would come at his call from the high treetops, and the saint would take it in his hand and set it on his shoulder, and it would be running in and out of the folds of the hood of his habit. And this the bishop said he had often seen.

CUTHBERT OF LINDISFARNE

ST. CUTHBERT IS NORTHERN ENGLAND'S most popular saint; his life was written by the great storyteller Bede the Venerable, whose grave is not far from Cuthbert's in Durham Cathedral. Cuthbert was a monk and bishop of Lindisfarne (Holy Island, as it is called), off the northeast coast of England. Both Durham and Lindisfarne are still very popular destinations of thousands of pilgrims each year. Little is known about Cuthbert's early life, but he was probably born into an Anglo-Saxon family about 634 CE in southern Scotland. Despite his Saxon origins, he was very much a Celt by temperament, and deeply influenced by Celtic spirituality. In 651, he joined the monastery at Melrose, on the Scottish border, which had been founded by Aidan (d. 651), an Irish monk from Columcille's monastery at Iona. Thus began a long life of intense pastoral involvement, serving as a guestmaster at Ripon and prior at Lindisfarne, before moving to Inner Farne Island, not far from Lindisfarne, where he attempted to live as a solitaire. Unfortunately for Cuthbert, great numbers of people sought him out for spiritual guidance. In 684, against his own wishes, he was elected a bishop, but only agreed to accept that office after the king himself had sailed to Inner Farne and begged him to do so. The following year, Cuthbert was consecrated bishop of Lindisfarne, and once again assumed a very active ministry. In 687, he resigned as bishop and returned to his beloved Inner Farne, where he died. His was a life, it seems, torn between his love of people and his passion for solitude. Like Patrick and Brigit too, Cuthbert shepherded sheep as a youth, and several of Bede's stories about him reflect his love of animals, and their love for him. Islands located near Inner Farne are the home today of numerous seals that bark to each other and to the passing boats of pilgrims seeking to visit the holy place.

Cuthbert's feast day is March 20.

Cuthbert's Fasting, and His Sharing Food with His "Comrade"

While Cuthbert was considering entering a monastery and was traveling alone, he turned at the third hour of the day (9:00 a.m.) into a village some distance away that he happened upon by chance. And he entered the house of a certain religious housewife, wishing to rest there a little and intending to ask for food for the horse on which he was riding, rather than for himself, for it was the beginning of the winter season. The woman received him kindly and earnestly begged him to allow her to prepare him a morning meal to refresh him. The man of God refused saying, "I cannot eat yet because it is a fast day." For it was Friday, a day on which most of the faithful are accustomed to extending their fast until the ninth hour (3:00 p.m.) out of reverence for the passion of the Lord. The woman, being given to hospitality, persisted, saying, "Look, you will find no village and no human habitation on the road you are taking; and you have a long journey before you, which you cannot finish before sunset. So I pray you to accept food before you set out." Though she urged him, his own love of religion overcame the urgency of her entreaty, and he set out once more fasting, and fasted the whole day until evening. When evening was at hand, he discovered that he could not finish the journey and that there were no lodgings in the neighborhood. Suddenly he saw some shepherds' huts close by, which had been roughly built during the summertime and were then lying open and deserted. He entered one in order to find shelter there, and tying the horse he had been riding to the wall, he collected a bundle of straw that the wind had removed from the roof and gave it to the horse to eat. He himself began to pray, when suddenly in the midst of his psalm-singing, he saw the horse lift up its head, seize the thatching of the house with its mouth and drag it down. Amid the straw falling from the roof, Cuthbert saw a folded cloth fall as well. Wishing to discover more certainly what it was, he drew near when his prayer was finished, and found, wrapped in the cloth, half a loaf of bread still warm, and some meat, enough for one meal for himself. Then he uttered praises, thanking God "who has deigned to provide a supper for me who am fasting out of love for Him, and also for my comrade." So he divided the piece of bread that he had found and gave half of it to the horse and the rest he kept for his own food. From that day he became readier than ever to fast, because indeed he understood clearly that his food had been provided for him in a solitary place, by the gift of him who once for many days fed the prophet Elijah in the desert with the food brought through the ministrations of birds, there being no man there to minister to him.

His Good Friend the Eagle's Ministry

Now on a certain day Cuthbert had left the monastery to preach, as he so often did, accompanied by only a youth. They were already tired with the long journey they had been on, and no little distance still remained before they would reach the village for which they were headed. The saint said to the boy, in order to test him, "Come, tell me, comrade, where do you intend to refresh yourself today? Or have you any resource on the way to whom you can turn?" The boy answered, "I have long been silently pondering that matter in my heart; for we have brought with us no provisions for the journey, nor do we have anyone we know on the way who will receive us hospitably, and a great part of the journey remains that we cannot complete without suffering—if we continue our fasting." Then the man of God replied, "Learn, my dear son, always to have faith and trust in the Lord, for he who serves God faithfully never perishes of hunger." And, looking up, he saw an eagle flying above them. "Do you see that eagle flying far off?" he asked the boy, "It is possible for God to refresh us today with that eagle's assistance." With such words they went on their way along a certain river when suddenly they saw the eagle settling on the bank. The man of God asked, "Do you see where our friend, as I foretold, is settling? Run, I beg you and see what food she has brought us from the Lord and bring it quickly here." The boy ran up and brought back a large fish that the eagle had just taken from the river. But the man of God asked again, "What have you done, my son? Why have you not given our handmaiden *her* share? Cut it quickly in half and take her the share that she deserves for ministering to us." The boy did as he was told and carried the rest with him. When the time for eating arrived, they turned into the next village, and giving the portion of the fish to be broiled that they still had, they refreshed themselves and those into whose house they entered. Then Cuthbert preached the word of God to them and praised him for his gifts, for "blessed is the person whose hope is in the name of the Lord and who has not looked after vanity nor idle folly." And so they resumed their journey, setting out to reach those whom they hoped to teach.

How Otters Warmed St. Cuthbert's Feet

Inside the monastery the man of God performed more and more signs and wonders, and his reputation increased. A certain nun called Aebbe, who was in charge of the convent of Coldingham, was honored for both her piety and her nobility, for she was King Oswy's sister. One day she sent a message to Cuthbert asking if he would come and exhort the community. The holy man came and stayed a few days, showing them the way of salvation in deed and in word. It was his custom to rise in the dead of night, while everyone else was sleeping, and to go out and pray, returning just in time for morning prayers. One night a monk watched him sneak out, and then secretly followed him to see where he was going and what he was about. Cuthbert went down toward the beach below the monastery and out into the sea until he was up to his arms and neck in deep water. Waves splashed all during his vigil throughout the dark hours of the night. At daybreak Cuthbert came out of the water, knelt down on the sand, and prayed. Suddenly two otters jumped out of the sea, stretched themselves out before him, warmed his feet with their breath, and even tried to dry him with their fur. When they had finished, they received his blessing and slipped back to their watery home. Soon he was home and back in choir with the rest of the monks at the proper time.

DAVID OF WALES

DAVID (OR *DEWI SANT* as the Welsh call him) is the patron saint of Wales, and according to more recent recognition due to his lifestyle and diet, of vegans and vegetarians. He was born about 520 CE, the son of Sanctus, a Welsh king, and Non, one of the great female saints of the early Celtic Church. He became founder of numerous monasteries, including that called *Cell Muine* in the southwestern corner of Wales, where the great Cathedral of St. David now stands. David appears in numerous Celtic hagiographies as a soul friend and mentor of many saints, including Maedoc of Ferns, protector of wolves, and Modomnoc, patron saint of bees and beekeepers. Other famous Irish monastic founders who visited him in his monastery were Finnian of Clonard, Senan of Scattery Island, Finbarr of Cork, and Brendan of Clonfert. He was nicknamed "the Water-man," probably because of the strict monastic rule, including abstinence from alcohol and the drinking of water only, which he enforced at his Welsh monastery. David and his fellow-monks also maintained a diet of bread and vegetables, with just a sprinkling of salt, evidently so as not to inflict unnecessary suffering upon any creature by taking its life for food. This respect for animals also was manifest in their preferring to do hard manual labor themselves rather than to use cattle or oxen to help them plow the fields. At the time of his death in 589 or 601 (historians disagree), his last words to his monks and townspeople were, "Be joyful brothers and sisters. Keep your faith and do the little things that you have seen and learned from me."

David's feast day is March 1.

Prophecy of David's Greatness, through a Stag, Fish, and Hive of Bees

Although the Lord has loved and known his own before ever he created the world, there are some whom he makes known beforehand by many signs and revelations. Consequently, that saint who was named David in his baptism but "Dewi" by the common people was not only fore-told by authentic prophecies of angels thirty years before his birth (first to his father, and then to St. Patrick), but was also proclaimed as one who was enriched with mystic gifts and endowments.

On a certain occasion, his father, Sanctus by name and merits, and in full enjoyment of royal power over the people of Ceredigion, heard in a dream the voice of an angel: "Tomorrow you will awake and go hunting. You will kill a stag near the river, and in that place you will find three gifts, namely, the stag which you will pursue, a fish, and a hive of bees. Now, of these three, you will set aside the honeycomb and a portion of the fish and of the stag. These you will send to Maucannus's monastery, there to be preserved for a son who will be born of you." These three gifts foreshadowed David's life. The honeycomb declared his wisdom, for just as the honey lies embedded in the wax, so he perceived the spiritual meaning within a literal statement. The fish proclaimed his abstinence, for, as the fish lives by water, so David rejected wine, fermented liquor, and everything intoxicating, and led a blessed life for God on bread and water only; thus, he was called "David who lives on water." The stag signified power over the ancient serpent. For as the stag, after feeding on the snakes that it has destroyed, longs for a spring of water, so David selected his own well of life with a ceaseless flow of tears.

David Founds Monasteries Whose Monks Worked with Feet and Hand

David founded twelve monasteries in all. First he reached Glaston-bury in England and built a church. Next he went to Bath, where he changed the foul water to healthy by blessing it, endowing it with a continuous heat that made it suitable for the bathing of bodies. One day his three most faithful disciples came to David. They were accompanied by a group of their fellow-disciples. One in mind and heart, they went to a place previously foretold by an angel where, in the name of God, they lit a fire. There at Menevia on the site that the angel had previously shown them, the community in the Lord's name built a noble monastery. When this was all completed, such an asceticism did the holy father decree that every monk toiled at daily labor, and spent his life working with his hands for the community. Knowing that idle rest was the source and the mother of vices, he bowed down the shoulders of the monks with pious labors, for those who give into idleness develop a spirit of instability and apathy with restless lustful urges. David's monks eagerly worked with feet and hands. They placed the yoke upon their shoulders, dug the earth unweariedly with mattocks and spades, and carried in their holy hands hoes and saws for cutting. With their own efforts, they provided for all the necessities of the community. Possessions they scorned, the gifts of the wicked they rejected, and riches they abhorred. They brought in no oxen to help themselves of the brethren. The work completed, no complaint was heard. When labor in a field was finished, they returned to the cloisters of the monastery and spent the whole of the day until the evening in reading, writing, or praying.

A Simple Vegetarian Diet in the Monastery

Everyone restored and refreshed his weary limbs by partaking of supper, but not to excess, for too much, though it be of bread alone, engenders self-indulgence. At meal, all took supper according to the varying conditions of their bodies or age. They did not serve courses of different flavor nor richer kinds of food: their food was, in fact, bread and herbs seasoned with salt, while they quenched a burning thirst with a temperate kind of drink. Besides, for either the sick, those advanced in age, or those wearied by a long journey, they provided some dishes of tastier food, since it was not proper to apportion to all in equal measure. When thanks had been given to God, they went to the church, and there they gave themselves up to prayer. Then they composed their limbs for sleep. In all things, they imitated the monks of the Egyptian desert and lived a life like theirs.

GALL OF ST. GALLEN

THE TWO GREAT IRISH MISSIONARIES, Columban and Gall, traveled from Ireland to the European continent, bringing the gospel message. Gall was probably born about 560 CE, and was placed at an early age at the monastery in Bangor, where he became Columban's pupil. Ordained a priest at the age of thirty, he set out with Columban for the Continent in 590. After Columban had founded three monasteries in France, the two friends traveled on to Germany, and then to the shores of Lake Zurich in Switzerland. There they settled down for two years. Gall was assigned important pastoral and liturgical responsibilities, as well as that of catching fish in the nearby lake for their suppers. Although he was a scholar and excellent preacher, Gall is more often associated with being fond of solitude, and especially of fishing. This is perhaps why he is often portrayed holding a fisherman's net in paintings and statues. He also is associated in art with a bear that is generally represented standing on its hind legs and carrying a log. Gall and Columban parted ways when the older man decided to continue his missionary travels into Italy. While Columban moved on to Bobbio, where he died and where a church now holds his remains in a beautiful marble tomb, Gall built a hermitage at the site that became the origins of the beautiful city St. Gallen. After Gall's death about 630, a Benedictine monastery was built that became one of the most famous centers of scholarship in Europe for over a thousand years. It also soon became a favorite place of pilgrimage because it contained Gall's relics. As the following stories show, St. Gall was helped by both a friendly bear and otters who came to his rescue in times of need.

Gall's feast day is celebrated October 16.

Gall, the Fisherman, and the Friendly Bear

Now Hiltibod, the deacon of the priest Willimar, was thoroughly familiar with every nook and cranny of the wilderness, for he loved to roam through it in order to catch fish and snare hawks. Through daily habit he had come to know its inmost recesses. Gall, increasingly admitting him into his friendship, asked him if he had ever found in the wilderness any spot abounding in pure, wholesome water, "For," he told Hiltibod, "I am filled with a burning desire to pass the days I have left on this earth in some retreat." The deacon replied, "This wilderness, my father, has many waters flowing through it, but it is a wild and fearsome place, full of high mountains with narrow winding glens and haunted by savage beasts. Besides stags and such harmless animals, it breeds countless bears and boars and wolves that are exceedingly fierce. Were I to lead you there, I fear they would devour you."

"The apostle Paul," rejoined the holy man, "has said, 'If God be for us, who can be against us,' and again, 'We know that all things work together for good to them that love God' [Rom 8:31, 28]. He who delivered Daniel from the lions' den can also save me from the clutches of wild beasts."

Then the deacon answered Gall, "Put some food into your satchel and the smallest of your fishing-nets. Tomorrow I will lead you into the wilderness. If you find in it a spot that suits you, give thanks to God. For God who has brought you from a far country will himself send his angel with us, even as He gave a companion from his servant Tobias, and will show us some spot suited to our pious desires." The saint, thus, remained fasting for the rest of that day and spent the night in prayer until the dawn. Then the athlete of God, taking with him the things his guide had told him, set out on his way after praying, with the deacon leading the way. They journeyed throughout the day, until they came to the stream called Steinaha, and followed its course until they reached the cliff from which descends the rushing water that forms a fine pool below.

Here they saw a quantity of fish and, throwing their nets into the water, they caught some. Then they kindled a fire, boiled the fish, and laid out the bread that they had brought. Gall retired at a short distance to pray. As he was walking through the tangled underbrush, his foot caught on something and he fell to the ground. The deacon ran to him, but the man of God, filled with the spirit of prophecy, said, "Let me be. This shall be my resting place forever; here will I dwell, for God has chosen it." And, after praying, Gall rose to his feet, and took a hazel twig, forming it into a cross, and fixed it in the ground.

While he was thus engaged, a bear came down from the mountains and began stealthily to pick up the crumbs and morsels that the two men had dropped. When Gall saw this, he said to the beast, "In the name of the Lord, I command you to take up a log and throw it on the fire." The bear turned at his command, brought a large log forward, and threw it into the fire. The deacon, in the meantime, pretending to be asleep, observed all of this. At last, he rose and threw himself at the saint's feet, saying, "Now I know truly that the Lord is with you, since even the beasts of the wilderness obey you." But the saint answered him, "Take heed that you tell no one of this until you see the glory of God."

Gall and the Helpful Otters

Sometime later, Euastasius, abbot of the monastery of Luxeuil in Gaul, who had been appointed by Columban of happy memory, passed from the exile of this life to the fatherland on high. The monks gathered and decided to recall Gall as abbot. They sent six of their number who had originally come from Ireland to bear him a letter setting forth their wishes. When they arrived at Gall's hermitage and presented the letter to him, he said to them, "My brothers, I left my kinsfolk and acquaintances and sought out the distant recesses of the wilderness so that I might have more leisure and freedom to serve the Lord. I have also refused the rank of bishop when it was offered to me, as well as the riches of the world. How, after giving up so much and embracing poverty, shall I again be entangled in the affairs of this life, uplifted by its honors and weighed down by its burdens? Far be it for me that having put my hand to the plough I should now look back on what I have left. You yourselves know that when I was among you, I always tried to be humble and obedient. Do you now try to encourage me to a position so exalted? No, make your plans anew, and turn elsewhere, for the Lord will not allow me to change the work I have now embraced."

Then he called one of his monks and asked what they were to have for their next meal. On hearing that there was only a small measure of flour for them all, he ordered them to make it into loaves and gather together some vegetables. Then he himself took his net and, accompanied by one of his disciples and the brethren who had just arrived, he went to the pool in the stream, saying, "Let us see whether the merciful Lord will grant us some little fishes for our needs."

On reaching the pool in which the waters of the stream were collected, they saw a big fish swimming in it, chased by two otters. They threw in their net, caught the fish, and brought it to land. The otters meanwhile plunged into the depths and drove such a multitude of fish into the net that it burst in several places. As soon as they had landed their catch, the saint said to the brethren, "It is because of your coming today that the Lord has given us this wondrous sign of his bounty." As they returned to the monastery, a man appeared who brought the saint as proof of his devotion two skins full of wine and three bushels of flour. These gifts were thankfully received, and all partook of the abundance of food. Gall kept his visitors for some days, and then dismissed them with the kiss of peace. Armed with his blessing, they returned home.

GOBNAIT OF BALLYVOURNEY

DESCRIBED IN AN EARLY MEDIEVAL text as "in God's love she was a complete treasure," Gobnait was born in Ireland in the seventh century. The name Gobnait is Irish for Abigail, meaning bringer of joy, but as the patron saint of beekeepers (along with Sts. Ambrose and Modomnoc), her name has been anglicized as Deborah, meaning honeybee. Most likely she was born in north Clare and may have been a descendant of Conaire the Great, king of Ireland. Her first hermitage was near the Cliffs of Moher, before she moved to Inis Oirr, the smallest of the Aran Islands. She later journeyed to Ballyvourney, where she became abbess of a monastery and stayed for the rest of her life. There are many stories of Gobnait, especially regarding her beekeeping. Renowned for her care of the sick, one story tells of how she cured a sick nun using her own honey. Many accounts tell of how she prevented invaders from carrying off her cattle, turning a beehive into a bronze helmet and the bees themselves into soldiers. Another version tells of how she let loose the bees from her hives and they attacked invaders who sought to harm Gobnait's community. It is this latter legend that inspired the Harry Clarke stained-glass window in the Honan Chapel at University College Cork. This window shows the saint dressed in royal blue robes with elaborate designs in turquoise. Gobnait wears a silver cloak and a veil. Her face is surrounded by bees, and at her feet she is portrayed as carrying a honeycomb while the bees are depicted chasing the thieves who threaten to rob her monastery. Gobnait is a very popular saint today in Ireland, with many pilgrims visiting Ballyvourney in County Cork. Other main centers of devotion to her are the Aran Islands and Dun Chaoin in West Kerry. The following story tells of how she found what was then called her "place of resurrection," the place many Celtic saints are in search of, where they will die and await, as Christians believe, the resurrection of their bodies. It is significant that deer become, as shown here, the guides to confirming that she had found the right place, since ancient Celtic lore associates the deer as symbolic of the soul. Celtic lore also believed that the soul left the body as a bee or a butterfly, and thus bees were held in high esteem. So it is not surprising that Gobnait added beekeeping to her life's work, developing a lifelong affinity for them.

Gobnait's feast day is February 11, two days before that of St. Modomnoc, the other Irish beekeeper.

Gobnait and the White Deer

Born in County Clare, Gobnait fled to the island of Inis Oirr in the Aran Islands, escaping from her father who was said to be a pirate. An angel had appeared to her and told her not to return to her father's ship, but rather to journey inland to a place where she would find nine white deer grazing, marking the place of her resurrection. So Gobnait traveled south in search of this place, traversing the Boggeragh Mountains, stopping near Macroon, where she saw three white deer. But this was not the prophesied number she was looking for, so she continued to Killeen. There she saw six deer; but, again, this did not fulfill the angel's words. She went further southward. Across the Sullane River and up a wooded hill she saw them: nine white deer grazing, as the angel had said she would. This was the spot called Gort na Tiobratan. Here she built for herself a simple cell and prayed in gratitude to God, who had led her to her place of resurrection. Young girls came to her, seeking to join her and create a community. They herded sheep and cows, made butter and bread, and kept a hive of bees. Along with the honey, vegetables and wild berries were their daily diet, and each evening they shared their main meal. This little community was part of the larger, surrounding community at Ballyvourney, to which Gobnait and her nuns ministered, especially to the sick or those in need. Loved by many, this is where she died, and was buried to await her resurrection.

GODRIC OF FINCHALE

GODRIC WAS AN ENGLISH HERMIT, merchant, and popular medieval saint who lived from 1065 to 1170. He was born in Walpole in Norfolk and died in Finchale in County Durham. Several hagiographies are extant, the most important one written by his contemporary, a monk named Reginald of Durham. Godric was said to have been born into a poor family, "slender in rank and wealth, but abundant in righteousness and virtue." First a peddler, then a sailor, he may even have been the captain and owner of a ship. After years at sea, Godric went to the island of Lindisfarne, the "holy isle" off the coast of England where St. Cuthbert had lived. There he encountered Cuthbert—not a physical encounter since Cuthbert had been long dead and interred at Durham Cathedral—but a spiritual meeting with the saint that changed his life. So impressed was he with the saint that he fell to his knees one day and begged God for the grace to be able to be like Cuthbert. Following this, Godric began to devote his life to Christianity and service to God. After many pilgrimages, including one to Santiago de Compostela, he returned to England and lived with an elderly hermit named Aelric for two years. When the hermit died, Godric made one last pilgrimage to Jerusalem, and then returned home where he convinced the bishop of Durham to grant him a place to live as a hermit at Finchale, by the River Wear. He was led to the site of his hermitage by a vision of St. Cuthbert; he lived there for the final sixty years of his life. As time passed, his reputation for holiness and wisdom grew, and many people sought him out for his advice, including Aelred of Rievaulx, Thomas Becket, and even Pope Alexander III. Godric was also a composer of music, the oldest surviving songs in English for which the original musical settings survive. He is, however, perhaps best remembered for his kindness toward animals, and many stories recall his protection of the creatures who lived near his home in the woods.

Godric's feast day is May 21.

Godric's Garden and the Wild Deer

Now if one is intent too long upon one task, the mind in tedium very soon revolts against its undertaking: and so Godric, the man of God, would turn the energy of his mind to various activities, yet seldom did he suspend his soul from prayer. He had rooted up from the ground nearby the undergrowth of the forest, and now began upon the tree trunks that were left to graft in cuttings of fruit trees that he had obtained from his visitors. Very skillful he was, and he made for himself a kind of enclosed orchard. In summer, when the tender shoots came to life again with green leaves, the branches he had grafted in began to swell and gradually here and there fragile sprays of green and young leaves appeared. But the unaccustomed sweetness of them was very tempting to the wild things of the woods, and they began very greedily to crop this strange new green-ness, and most assiduous they were in visiting this agreeable pasture. They would nip off the sprays of the apple boughs and gnaw the tender juicy bark and scatter with their hooves the young saplings. Not a single kind of tree, of those he had grafted with so much care, did these wild creatures of the forest allow to come to maturity.

One day, coming out of his hermitage, he saw a wild stag from the woods cropping the tender leaves of his trees, scattering and spoiling with all its heart. Approaching the creature, Godric bade it with a crook of his finger not to run away from that spot, but to wait until he got there, without stirring. Oh strange and stupendous mystery! The stag, this wild thing of the woods that knew no discretion, understood the will of the man of God from his gesture alone, and standing still it began trembling all over, as if it knew that it had offended the soul of the man of God. Its extreme tremor and fear went to Godric's heart, and he checked his anger and the blows he had meant to inflict. The stag dropped on its knees as he came, and bowed its head, to ask pardon as best it could for its bold trespass.

Godric ungirt his belt and put it around the neck of the kneeling animal, and so led him beyond the bounds of his orchard, and there releasing him told him to go free and wander wherever he wanted.

The Irksome Hare versus Godric's Concern for the Poor

Godric had planted vegetables in his garden to feed the poor, and these a little hare used stealthily to devour. The holy man put up with the damage for a long time, but finally his patience ran out. At last the track of the hare's paws gave it away. Godric came upon the thief in his garden, and as it turned in headlong flight, he ordered it to stop. The poor little creature stopped and awaited in trembling and alarm the arrival of its pursuer. The saint caught it, struck it with his rod, and ordered the hare, "See to it that neither you nor any of your acquaintances come to this place again, nor dare to encroach on what was meant for the needs of the poor." Still, with this order, Godric tied a bundle of vegetables on the hare's shoulders and sent it off for later consumption.

The Gentleness of Godric's Heart

The gentleness of the saint's heart was not only reflected in his kindness to people, but his wise solicitude for the very reptiles and creatures of the earth. For in winter when all about was frozen in the cold, he would go out barefoot. If he came upon any animal helpless with the misery caused by the cold, he would cuddle it under his armpit or in his bosom to warm it. Many times would the kind Godric go looking under the thick hedges or tangled patches of briars, and if he happened to find a creature that had lost its way, or been harmed by the harshness of the weather, or was tired, or was half-dead, he would recover it with all the healing art he had. And if anyone in his service had caught a bird or little beast in a snare or a trap or a noose, as soon as he found it, he would snatch it from their hands and let it go free in the fields or the woods. Many times they would hide their captive spoils under a corn measure or a basket or some secret hiding place, but even so, they could never deceive Godric or keep it hidden from him. For often without any saying a thing, and indeed with those disavowing and protesting, he would go straight to the place where the creatures had been hidden. While they would stand by crimson-faced with fear and confusion, the holy man would lift them out of where they were being hidden and set them free. So, too, hares and other beasts fleeing from huntsmen he would take in, and house them in his hut. When anyone hunting their catch was gone, he would send the animals away to their familiar haunts. Many times the creatures of the forest would run away from the huntsmen who lay in wait for them, and take shelter in the safety of Godric's hut. They knew that a sure and safe refuge was provided for them there.

ITA OF KILLEEDY

ITA (ALSO ITE OR IDE) IS, after Brigit, the most famous of Irish female saints. Her hagiographer even describes her as "a second Brigit." A sixth-century abbess, Ita founded a monastery in County Limerick at Killeedy (which means "cell or church of Ita"). She came from the highly respected clan of the Deisi, and her family raised horses that Ita cared for as a child. While she loved her family and the animals, when she became a young woman she discerned her calling to be a nun. Her father, like Brigit's, however, was resistant, but eventually, with the help of her mother and her own prayers, she was able to get his permission. Ita then left home and settled at the foot of Sliabh Luchra, where other women from neighboring clans soon joined her. There she founded a monastic school for the education of boys, one of whom was Brendan of Clonfert. Tradition says that the two became soul friends. Ita herself had many students, besides Brendan, for she is called the "Foster Mother of the Saints of Erin." Besides her significant mentoring, she is associated with competence in healing, guided as shamans are, by her dreams. Ita was also a powerful female confessor in the early Celtic Church who was not afraid of giving penances and yet at the same time was especially compassionate and forgiving. She also continued to be a lover of animals, not only horses but a special mule.

Ita's feast day is January 15.

Ita's Qualities as a Child and Her Dream

Ita performed many miracles while she was yet a small child, and once she could speak and walk, she was prudent, very generous, and mild toward everyone, human and animal alike. She consistently attempted to overcome evil, and always did what she could to promote good. One night when she was sleeping, Ita saw an angel of the Lord approach her and give her three precious stones. When she awoke, she did not know what that dream signified, and she had a question in her heart about it. Then an angel appeared to her and said, "Why are you wondering about that dream? These three precious stones you saw being given to you signify the coming of the Blessed Trinity to you, Father, Son, and Holy Spirit. Always in your sleep and vigils the angels of God and holy visions will come to you, for you are a temple of God, in body and soul." After saying this, the angel left her.

Her Advice as St. Brendan's Soul Friend

St. Brendan once asked Ita what three works were most pleasing to God, and what three works were most displeasing to God. Ita answered, "Three things that please God most are true faith in God with a pure heart, a simple life with a grateful spirit, and generosity inspired by charity. The three things that most displease God are a mouth that hates people, a heart that harbors resentments, and confidence in wealth." St. Brendan and all who were there, hearing that advice, glorified God in his chosen one.

A Rich Man's Desire for Red and White Colts

One time a rich man of the world came to Ita, knowing of her knowledge of horses, and said to her, "I ask you, holy one of God, that my mares will bear colts this year with red coloring and white heads." Ita replied, "That is not in my limited power to do what you ask. It is for God to use his elements as he wishes." Then the rich man asked her to intercede for him with God, saying, "As the Father and Son and Holy Spirit, the triune and one God of heaven and earth, of sea and of all humans, who gave colors to nature, clothes, and animals too, pray that he make the colors of my colts, as I desire." Moved by his faith and his persistence, Ita said to him, "Since you believe in this way in God, so will your colts be this year as you wish." The rich man went off delighted with that prophecy. And all happened to him as Ita had said.

Ita's Special Donkey

Ita was the proud owner of a very special donkey. It was said that all the milk that was used in her convent was brought there by the donkey every day from the dairy on the northern slope of a hill called Seeconglas, four miles southwest of Killeedy. One day as the poor beast was passing through a nearby town with his accustomed burden, a cruel-hearted man attacked him with dogs. The donkey, fleeing from his pursuers, jumped across the river that flows by the townland, leaving the impress of his hooves on a ledge of rock that can still be seen today. When St. Ita saw the donkey on his arrival, all torn and bleeding, in her anger she cursed the place where the outrage was committed. Another time while Ita was out riding her donkey it became lame by stepping on a thorn on the road. Stopping immediately when she saw that her poor animal had begun to limp, she removed the thorn from the donkey's hoof. This very thorn then grew into a tree whose thorns turned downward and were therefore innocuous, not troubling any creatures thereafter.

KEVIN OF GLENDALOUGH

KEVIN STANDS IN THE FOREFRONT of the great company of Irish saints. One of Ireland's abbots of a monastery who was not a bishop but an ordinary priest, he was born sometime in the sixth century in the province of Leinster. As was true of many young people, including Hildegard of Bingen and the Venerable Bede, Kevin at the age of seven was sent to a monastery to be educated by monks. When he decided to be ordained, he wanted to live as a hermit, however, rather than remain in a monastic community. An angel, it is said, led him to a location in the Valley of the Two Lakes, near Glendalough, where he lived for seven years, clad only in animal skins and sleeping on a stone at the water's edge. Considering the numerous stories about animals that appear in his Life and his obvious love of them, it is no wonder that he chose not to eat any meat, living on a very frugal vegetarian diet of only nuts, berries, and herbs. His reputation for holiness eventually attracted other monks who begged Kevin to leave his solitary life and be their spiritual leader. The monastery that was built at Glendalough eventually became a monastic city whose ruins are still viewed today by pilgrims and tourists alike. Kevin's love of animals led the local people to recognize his abilities as a veterinarian, and they started bringing sick animals to him, many of whom seemed to be miraculously cured by his touch. So many legends are told about his great love of nature that he is often called the Irish Francis of Assisi. Stories about him suggest that he and his community provided sanctuary in their monastery to both wild creatures and tame. The most famous story is his compassion for a mother blackbird or raven that reveals his patience, gentleness, and stamina.

Kevin's feast day is June 3.

Kevin, the Hermit, and the Helpful Otter

After Kevin was ordained, an angel told him to go into the desert glen. As he was setting out, the angel came to guide him to the crags that are on the western side of the two lakes in Glendalough. There he had no food but the nuts of the forest, the herbs of the earth, and fresh water for drinking. He did not even have a cell in which to live. He would often go to the crag and to the cave called "Kevin's Bed," and he would pray long and fervently to God. For seven years he followed this solitary routine, far from the companionship of others. One time, after Kevin had been in his place of solitude for a while, he went into the lake at the end of a snowy night, as was his custom. As he was reciting his psalms the book fell into the lake and sank to some depths. An angel came and said, "Do not grieve." Soon an otter swam up from the bottom of the lake with his book in its mouth and gave it to Kevin. Not a line nor letter was blotched or blotted. The angel then told him to return to society to teach and preach the word of God, and not hide himself any longer.

Kevin's Compassion for a Blackbird

All of his life, because of the severity of his asceticism, Kevin was accustomed to spend every Lent in a wattled hut, with a grey flagstone under him as a bed. His only food was the music of the angels. Living in this way, he would spend six weeks there. One Lent a blackbird came from the woods to his hut and hopped on his palm as he lay on the flagstone with his hand stretched out. Kevin kept his hand in that position, so that the blackbird could build its nest in it. He remained there until she had hatched her brood. An angel came to visit Kevin and ordered him to stop the penance in which he was then engaged and to return to society once more. "It is no great thing for me to bear this pain of holding my hand under the blackbird for the sake of heaven's King," Kevin said, "for upon the Cross of suffering Jesus bore every pain on behalf of Adam's offspring." "Come out of the hut," the angel insisted. "I will not come," said he, and stayed until the chicks had hatched.

Kevin Saves a Wild Boar

Another time some hunters were hunting a wild boar with their dogs in hot pursuit. As soon as the boar perceived the dogs near him, he set off down the slope of the glen to seek Kevin's protection. Kevin protected the boar and commanded the dogs to stop following him. As he did so, the feet of the dogs stuck to the ground, so that they could not move in any direction. Shortly after this, the hunters came into Kevin's presence, and on seeing their dogs fastened to the ground and the boar under Kevin's protection, they were astonished and filled with wonder at this miracle. Humbly and penitently, they asked Kevin to release their dogs, and promised him that they would never again pursue this boar. So Kevin let the boar run to the forest, and the name of God was glorified. Kevin was like this all his life, working miracles until he died at an advanced age of 129 years.

MÆDOC OF FERNS

MAEDOC WAS BORN IN IRELAND on an island in County Cavan about 558 CE and is considered the founder of Irish monasteries at Fern in County Wexford, at Drumlane in County Cavan, and Rossinver in County Leitrim. Maedoc is said to have been educated at St. David's school in Wales, and tradition has it that David and Maedoc were very close friends, with David dying in the arms of his friend and former pupil. Clearly, Maedoc had, like the other Celtic saints, a great capacity for making friends. Besides David, Maedoc had close ties with Molaise of Devenish (probably his closest friend), with Columcille (a colleague), Ita of Killeedy, and even Brigit of Kildare. Besides being a good soul friend, the portrait of Maedoc that emerges in his hagiography is that of a powerful saint with a strong intuition, and a great sensitivity toward those in pain. He is named, as many Native Americans are, after an aspect of nature: "son of star," a poetic title of honor. He is portrayed in the stories about him as close to nature and a friend of many kinds of animals, landing back in Ireland after his schooling in Wales with beehives, for example, and protecting a stag being pursued by hounds. But Maedoc seems to have especially enjoyed the company of wolves. Perhaps he even danced with them!

Maedoc's feast day is January 31.

Trees Falling and a Stag Protected

Maedoc and Molaise were comrades who loved each other very much. One day they sat praying at the foot of two trees. "Ah, Jesus!" they cried, "is it your will that we should part, or that we should remain together until we die?" Then one of the two trees fell to the south, and the other to the north. "By the fall of the trees," they said, "it is clear that we must part."

78

Then they told each other goodbye and kissed each other affectionately. Maedoc went to the south and built the noble monastery at Ferns in the center of Leinster, and Molaise went north to Lough Erne, and built a fair monastery at Devenish. Another day, when Maedoc was praying deep in the forest, he saw a stag pursued by hounds. The stag stopped by him, and Maedoc threw the corner of his cloak over its horns to protect it from the hounds. When they came running by, they could neither see nor smell the stag, and after they had gone, it ran for safety back into the forest.

Maedoc Walks on Water and Shows Compassion for Wolves

One day when Maedoc was walking by the ocean with his comrades, he said to them, "I am sorry that I did not ask my master, David, who should be my soul friend in Ireland." His disciples began to prepare a ship, but the boatmen were not willing to return to Wales. Maedoc leapt out of the boat and walked from wave to wave until an angel met him. "You need no soul friend but the God of the Elements," the angel said, "for He understands the thoughts and secrets of every person." So Maedoc built a church in that place called Oak-wood Hermitage, and settled there with his disciples. The brothers had two cows and a calf in the community. One day Maedoc was alone in his cell when he saw some wolves approaching. They circled him gently, and he understood that they were asking for food. He was moved to compassion for them and gave the calf to them to eat. But one of the brothers said to him, "Maedoc, the cows will not give milk without the calf." Maedoc said to him, "Bend your head towards me so that I may bless it; for when the cows see it, they will give their milk obediently to you." And so it was that whenever the cows saw the head of the brother, they would suddenly lick it, and then give their milk to him.

The Starving Mother Wolf and the Miracle of a Loaf and a Fish

On another occasion when Maedoc came to the monastery named Shanbo, at the foot of the hill called Mount Leinster, as he was going along the road a mother wolf, wretched, weak, and starving, happened to meet him. It came up to him gently as if seeking his attention. Maedoc asked a lad who had joined him on the road whether he had anything he could give the wolf. The boy said that he had only one loaf and a piece of fish. Maedoc took this from him and threw it to the wolf who hungrily ate the food. The boy was disturbed at seeing this and told the saint that he was afraid of what his master would do to him. Maedoc said, "Bring me some of the leaves of the forest." The boy did as he had been told. Then Maedoc blessed the foliage, and it was turned into a loaf and a fish, which he gave to the lad, making both wolf and lad happy.

MELANGELL OF NORTH POWYS

IRISH MISSIONARIES AND WANDERING monks brought Christianity to many parts of Europe in the early Middle Ages, from such Celtic lands as Brittany and Wales to Italy and other parts of the Continent. Some of them came to evangelize, others to minister to the pastoral needs of the Irish who had already settled there. The Irish were known for their wandering and later for going on numerous pilgrimages to holy sites. As the medieval writer, Walafrid Strabo (c. 808–49), said, "The custom of traveling to foreign lands has now become almost second nature to them." Some of these Irish traveled simply seeking solitude. St. Melangell, the daughter of an Irish prince who lived in the early seventh century CE, was one of those in search of a solitary life. Apparently, the only purpose of her travel to Wales from Ireland was to find a quiet place to pray. Little is known about her except that when a local prince was out hunting rabbits with his dogs, this saintly woman protected one of the poor rabbits by hiding it beneath her dress. Because of her compassion, the prince made her, as the following stories show, a wonderful gift. She remained in that place for thirty-seven years, and because of her protection of the rabbits, became known as the patron saint of hares and other small animals. Her site in Wales, Pennant Melangell, is today as popular a place of pilgrimage as it was in medieval times. Anglican Canon A. M. (Donald) Allchin calls her site one of the "thin places" where there is "the intersection of the timeless with time, where God's peace and eternity make their presence felt."

Today, St. Melangell is also identified as the patron saint not only of small animals in Wales but all of nature. Her feast day is May 27.

A Royal Hunt

In Powys there was once a certain most illustrious prince by the name of Brychwel Ysgithrog. This man was the Earl of Chester who at that time lived in the town of Pengwern Powys, which means "the head of Powys marsh." Now that very same noble prince gave his home for the use of God as an act of almsgiving both by his own free will and out of a sense of religious duty, making a perpetual grant of it for his own sake and for the sake of his heirs. One day in the year of our Lord 604, this prince went hunting in a certain place in Britain called Pennant, in the principality of Powys. When the hunting dogs of the prince came upon a hare, the dogs pursued it. The prince too gave chase until he came to a certain thicket of brambles that was large and full of thorns. In this thicket he found a girl of beautiful appearance who, given up to divine contemplation, was praying with the greatest devotion, with the hare lying boldly and fearlessly under the hem of her garments, its face toward the dogs.

Then the prince cried, "Get it, hounds, get it!" But the more he shouted, urging them on, the further the dogs retreated. Howling, they fled from the little animal. Finally, the prince, altogether astonished, asked the girl how long she had lived on her own on his lands, in such a lonely spot. In reply the girl said that she had not seen a human face for the past fifteen years. Then he asked the girl who she was, her place of birth and origins. In all humility, she answered that she was the daughter of King Jowchel of Ireland and that "because my father had intended me to be the wife of a certain great and generous Irishman, I fled from my native soil and with God leading me came here in order that I might serve God and the immaculate Virgin with my heart and pure body until my dying day." When the prince asked the girl her name, she replied that her name was Melangell.

A Sanctuary Given in Melangell's Name

Then the prince, considering in his innermost heart the flourishing though solitary state of the girl, said,

Melangell of North Powys

O most worthy virgin Melangell, I find that you are a handmaid of the true God and a most sincere follower of Christ. Therefore, because it has pleased the highest and all-powerful God to give refuge, for your merits, to this little wild hare with safe conduct and protection from the attack and pursuit of these savage and violent dogs, I give and present to you most willingly these my lands for the service of God. I do so that they may be a perpetual asylum, refuge, and defense in honor of your name, excellent girl. Let neither king nor prince seek to be so rash or bold toward God that they presume to drag away any man or woman who has escaped here, desiring to enjoy protection in these your lands, as long as they in no way contaminate or pollute your sanctuary or asylum. But, on the other hand, if any wrongdoer who enjoys the protection of your sanctuary shall set out in any direction to do harm, then the independent abbots of your sanctuary, who alone know of their crimes, shall ensure, if they find them in that place, that the culprits be released and handed over to the Powys authorities in order to be punished.

The virgin Melangell, who was so very pleasing to God, led her solitary life, as stated above, for thirty-seven years in this very same place. And the hares, which are little wild creatures, surrounded her every day of her life just as if they had been tame or domesticated animals. Nor, by the aid of divine mercy, were miracles and various other signs lacking for those who called upon her help and the grace of her favor with an inner motion of the heart. After the prince had told her this, that place called Pennant Melangell became a perpetual sanctuary, refuge, and safe haven for the oppressed, humans and animals alike. The same virgin, Melangell, worked to establish and instruct certain virgins who joined her with all concern and care in the same region in order that they might persevere and live in a holy and modest manner in the love of God, doing nothing else by day and by night.

MODOMNOC OF OSSORY

THE ORIGINAL CELTIC NAME of this holy man was Domnoc, to which was added, as happened with Irish saints who were held in high affection, the word *mo*, meaning "my"; hence the name Domnoc was changed to Modomnoc. This saint was an Irish missionary from present-day County Kilkenny who left Ireland to train for the priesthood with the famous St. David at Menevia in Wales. All those who resided in the monastic community there were expected to share in the manual work as well as the study and worship. His assignment was to care for the bees that were kept both for their honey and the production of mead. One of the best-known stories about him concerns his work as a beekeeper, especially his apparent ability to converse with them. This Irish folklore custom is called "telling the bees," and is said to ensure that bees not feel any offense due to exclusion from family affairs, and so will remain with the hive. It was believed that if one didn't tell the bees of a wedding, a birth, or a death, they would be "put into mourning" and a penalty would be paid: the bees might leave their hive, stop producing honey, or die. This custom of conversing with bees has been recognized in England, Ireland, Wales, Germany, Netherlands, France, Switzerland, and even the United States. It is artistically depicted by Charles Napier Hemy (1841–1917) in his painting, "Telling the Bees." Because of Modomnoc's care for his bees and his loving attention to talking with them, he became known, along with St. Gobnait, as the patron saint of bees and beekeepers. Bees were highly valued by the early church fathers, too, such as St. Ambrose and St. John Chrystostom, who said, "The bee is more honored than other animals, not because she labors, but because she labors for others." Modomnoc may have been aware of that saying. He is specifically remembered in the *Felire*

Oengusso: "In a little boat, from the east, over the pure-colored sea, my Domnoc brought the gifted race of Ireland's bees."

Modomnoc died in 550, and his feast day is February 13.

Modomnoc "Telling the Bees"

When Modomnoc was given charge of the bees, he planted the kinds of flowers best loved by them in a sheltered corner of the monastery garden. He talked to the bees as he worked among them, and they buzzed around his head in clouds as if they were responding. He would walk among the hives in the evening and talk to them, and the bees, for their part, would fly out of the hives to greet him. He was never stung by them. When the time came for Modomnoc to return to Ireland, three times the bees followed him in a great swarm and settled on the mast of the boat he was in. St. David perceived this unusual occurrence and interpreted it to be a good omen. He therefore allowed Modomnoc to bring the bees to Ireland. When he landed, Modomnoc built a church at a place called Bremore in County Dublin, and here he established the bees in a garden just like the one they had in Wales. He went on to serve God in the western part of the kingdom of Ossory, founding monasteries on the County Cork coast.

NINIAN OF WHITHORN

NINIAN IS SAID TO HAVE LIVED from 362 to 432 CE, and is considered to be the first apostle in Scotland, where he preached the gospel some time before Columcille arrived at Iona. He was the son of a converted chieftain of the Cumbrian Britons, studied at Rome, was ordained a priest, and then consecrated a bishop. Returning to evangelize his native Britain, he built a monastery at Whithorn in Galloway, on the southwestern coast of Scotland, which came to be known as *Candida Casa* (the White House), evidently because of its white stone. He and his monks used it as a base for their missionary work among the Picts in Scotland and Celts in Ireland. Our earliest authority on Ninian is Bede the Venerable (672–735), the first English historian who wrote about the saint some three hundred years after Ninian's death. More details of Ninian's life are provided by Aelred of Rievaulx (c. 1110–67) who had been brought up at the court of King David I of Scotland and wrote a Life of the saint.

Ninian's feast day is September 16.

The Prayer of Encirclement for the Protection of Animals

It sometimes pleased the most holy Ninian to visit his flocks and the huts of his shepherds, wishing that the flocks, which he had gathered together for the use of the monks, the poor, and pilgrims, should be beneficiaries of his blessing. Therefore, when all the animals were gathered together into one place, the servant of the Lord raised his hand and commended all that he had to the Divine protection. Going around them all and drawing as it were a little circle with the staff on which he leaned, he enclosed the cattle, commanding that all within that space should that night remain under God's protection. Having done all this, the man of God turned aside to rest for the night at the house of a certain honorable matron. When, after refreshing their bodies with food and their minds with the word of God, and all had gone to sleep, certain thieves appeared, and seeing that the cattle were neither enclosed by wall, nor protected by hedges nor kept in by a ditch, they looked to see if anyone was watching, or if anything else might resist their plans. When they saw that all was silent, and that nothing was present that by voice or movement or barking might frighten them, they rushed in and crossed the bounds that the saint had fixed for the cattle, wishing to carry them all off. But the Divine power was present, resisting the ungodly, casting them down, using against them brute beasts. For the bull of the herd rushed upon the men in fury, and striking at the leader of the thieves, threw him down, pierced his belly with his horns, killing the man. Meanwhile the saint, having finished the solemn service of prayer, went aside, and finding the man lying dead among the cattle, was moved with compassion and, turning to God, asked him to raise the dead. Nor did he stop crying tears and begging God's help. Then, truly, the power of Christ, because of the merit of the saint, restored to life the dead robber. Meanwhile the others, enclosed within the circle that the saint had made, seeing the servant of God, cast themselves with fear and trembling at his knees, begging his pardon. The saint then gave them his blessing, after chiding them for their evil plans, and granted them permission to depart.

PETROC OF PADSTOW

PETROC OF PADSTOW IS CONSIDERED Cornwall's most famous saint. No definite dates are given for his birth and death other than general reference to his living in the sixth century. Most likely he was born in south Wales. His hagiography says that Petroc studied in Ireland for twenty years before coming to Cornwall, landing at Haylemouth. From there he went to Lanwethinoc, now called Padstow, where he founded a monastery. Padstow (named after him—Petroc's Stow: the church of St. Petroc) was the principal center of his activities. About thirty years later, the holy man founded another monastery at Little Petherick. Like many of the Celtic saints, Petroc seems to have preferred the solitary life, living as a hermit on Bodmin Moor where he built a cell for himself by the river. Near the cell, another monastery housed the twelve comrades who had accompanied him there. Petroc died while on a visit to his monasteries, but his body was buried at Padstow. Like many Celtic saints, Petroc had a special affinity with wild animals and is often portrayed with a stag as his emblem—in memory of the one whom he sheltered from hunters. Petroc even healed the blindness of a great dragon, surely another creature who deserved compassion from the saint.

Petroc's feast day is celebrated on June 4.

In the Wilderness, Petroc Protects a Fleeing Stag

In Cornwall, Petroc appointed Father Peter, a most religious man whom he himself had received into the faith, as prior. Petroc then departed for the desert, taking with him only twelve whom he had chosen to dwell with him in the wilderness, among the valleys of the mountains, in a hiding

place of the rocks. On a certain day when the servant of God was praying alone in a place where he often prayed, he saw a stag appear in the
distance. It was fleeing toward him as hard as it could go, pursued by the
huntsmen of Constantine, a rich man, and his loudly barking dogs. The saint,
moved by compassion, protected the stag from being hurt. The stag was
being followed by Constantine himself, to whom his soldiers reported the
actions of Petroc. Constantine, full of wrath, would have hit the servant
of God with his sword, but was suddenly struck with paralysis, unable to
move hand or foot, until he sought pardon from the saint. Petitioned by
the soldiers, Petroc, through his prayers, healed the man. He then taught
Constantine and his nineteen soldiers the Christian faith and made them
gentle and kind, worshippers of Christ instead of fierce tyrants.

The Saint Heals a Dragon

So that the virtue of Petroc should be known even to "animals that
are not clean" (Gen 7:2), a great dragon that lived near the saint's cell in
the wilderness and was suffering from a piece of wood stuck in his right
eye, put aside his innate desire to harm people and hurried to the church
where Petroc was praying. Reclining his head on the outer threshold of
the building, he lay there for three days, waiting for a miracle from God.
By Petroc's command, he was sprinkled with water mixed with dust from
the pavement. Immediately, the wood was removed from his eye, and his
sight restored. Wonderful to tell, he then returned to his customary resting place.

SAMTHANN OF CLONBRONEY

SAMTHANN WAS AN IMPORTANT abbess of the monastery at Clonbroney in County Longford, Ireland. She was born in the second half of the seventh century. According to one tradition, she was distantly related to St. Patrick, who lived over two hundred years before her. Like St. Brigit, with whom she had much in common, many of Samthann's miracles concern food and accounts of her compassion and love of both animals and humans. We know little about her early life, except that she was born in Ulster and that her distinguished foster father was a king of Ireland. Also, unlike numerous other Irish female saints, Samthann was married before becoming a nun. When she entered the monastic community, her responsibilities included conducting the financial affairs of the monastery. This office evidently gave her the ability to be generous to lepers and guests, pilgrims and penitents who visited there, as well as members of her own community. Her many other abilities are expressed in the stories about her. She appears in dreams to offer direction and advice; she has a capacity to heal those who come to her for help; she goes into an ecstatic state while praying for the soul of a friend. Above all, Samthann is portrayed as a woman of prayer: someone who knocked frequently "at the doors of divine mercy."

Samthann died in 739 CE. Her feast day is December 19.

The Power of Samthann's Prayers regarding Beasts, Wild and Tame

A certain monk once questioned Samthann about how to pray. He wondered whether a person should pray lying down, sitting, or standing. She replied, "In every position, a person should pray." By the power of her prayers, St. Samthann tamed beasts of a pond near her monastery. They had previously caused havoc with people and the flocks, but, after that, they did no more harm. This same saint—with the help of only one cow— once fed fifty guests until they were completely satisfied. At the time she had nothing else with which to feed them. Having prayed, the holy virgin milked the cow and drew forth enough milk to quench the thirst of that number of people.

CONCLUSION

"WHAT IS MORE WONDERFUL than the incomparable tremendous story?" an Irish monk wrote back in the eleventh century, a thousand years ago. He clearly knew the power of stories to nourish the soul, to strengthen the heart, and to influence a person's behavior. Celtic hagiographers knew this too, and in telling the stories of their saints they sought to teach lessons, reinforcing a perspective that humans and animals are all related to one another, and that we are meant to enjoy each other's company as well as alleviate each other's pain.

The Lives of these Celtic saints constitute the largest body of hagiographies of any group in Christian history to have so many animal stories included in them. While Native American and Hawaiian peoples, as well as certain Asian spiritual traditions, have stories about animals, only the Celtic saints have so many references to them as fellow-creatures. This sense of kinship was an intrinsic aspect of Celtic Christian spirituality that affected not only those living in Celtic lands, but also significantly influenced later saints who were raised in geographical areas on the Continent, ministered to by Irish missionaries. The multitalented German mystic Hildegard of Bingen (1098–1179), for example, expresses her belief in the unity of all creation in the theology of greenness she developed as a theologian and writer. In the hagiography she wrote on St. Disibod, the Irish missionary and founder of her first monastery, she specifically shows her appreciation of the Irish contribution to her life. Francis of Assisi (1181–1226), as mentioned earlier, lived in a part of Italy where Christianity had been brought by the great Irish missionary St. Columban, and as a pilgrim he had visited his tomb in Bobbio. The numerous animal stories associated with Francis and his attitude of compassion toward animals and birds as "sisters" and "brothers" reflect the spirituality of the Celtic saints. In particular, his famous "Canticle of the Sun" expresses his love of all creatures great and small, and his seeing the entire cosmos, sun, moon, and all the stars as brothers and sisters too. Joan of Arc (1412–31), born in the part of France originally populated by the ancient Celts and raised in the tiny village of Domremy, which was visited by the Irish, speaks of a "Fairy Tree" where she and other children used to play while growing up, and her grandmother telling her stories of fairies. Joan, of course, epitomizes a Celtic shaman who hears voices and sees visions, and a Celtic female warrior who, while unusual in her own day, was common among early Celts, certainly a manifestation of what Carl Jung calls the Collective Unconscious that lived in her. She was also visited by saints, two of whom, Catherine and Michael, were favorites of Celtic Christians.

The stories in this book attest to the Celtic awareness, ancient and Christian, that all of life is interconnected. For Celtic Christians in particular, considering the prominence of this characteristic in their stories, it seems that, for them, one of the most significant criteria for sainthood itself was the compassionate treatment not only of human beings but of all creation, especially our fellow-creatures. Celtic hagiographers are, thus, suggesting to their readers that to be a holy person one must have this same type of relationship and awareness.

The stories told here allude to the sense of kinship the saints felt with animals, and their compassion toward them. Patrick saves a young deer from being slain by his own men; Brigit saves a hunted boar; Columcille manifests hospitality to a tired crane. Brendan recognizes a strange dog as a helpful guide and a whale as a place of shelter. Ciaran of Saighir welcomes a boar, a fox, a badger, a wolf, and a deer as his first monks. Kevin leaves his arms outstretched, giving a mother blackbird time for her chicks to hatch. So many of the saints are portrayed as helping the hunted, protecting them from harm. This act of saving animals being pursued by hunting dogs is a common storyline in the Lives of the Celtic saints: Maedoc throws his cloak over a stag pursued by hounds; Melangell hides a hunted hare beneath her skirt; Petroc protects yet another fleeing stag.

Of all the saints, only Godric is portrayed as impatient with wild animals. His reason, we recall, was his objection to the animals eating from his garden when the food was for the poor, he said, "not beasts." Even so, he was gentle as he led them away, putting up a fence to keep them out, and being solicitous even toward snakes! And the hagiographer reminds us, in winter, "when all about was frozen stiff in the cold, he would go out barefoot, and if he lighted on any animal helpless with misery of the cold, he would set it under his armpit or in his bosom to warm it....And if any-one in his service had caught a bird or little beast in a snare or a trap or a noose, as soon as he found it he would snatch it from their hands and let it go free in the fields or the glades of the wood." Though impatient with some, Godric obviously demonstrates an exceptional degree of compassion and love.

These are just a few of the things the saints did for animals. But the stories also show what animals did for them: the reciprocity that underlies so much *when we pay attention*—as the farmer does eventually with his pig in the movie *Babe*.

Ciaran of Clonmacnoise had a fox who acted as a sort of mail carrier between him and another monk. He also had a stag that used to visit him and on whose antlers he would allow Ciaran to place his books while the saint read. Ciaran of Saighir, as mentioned earlier, had his monastery built with the help of animals "as if they had been his monks"—perhaps the first ever of lay oblates or consociates increasingly popular today. St. Colman's monastic inhabitants—a rooster, a mouse, and a fly—ministered to him. As we recall from the earlier story, while the rooster acted as a sort of alarm clock, and the mouse would also wake him by gnawing at his clothes or nibbling at his ear, the third creature, a fly, would act as a marker on the page he was reading if Colman was called away. Still other animals provided comfort and compassion to the saints. Otters ministered to Cuthbert when he spent a night in the cold ocean waters praying, by warming his cold feet with their breath, even drying him with their fur. A bear helped Gall build a fire when the saint had twisted his ankle in a fall;

a white bird guided Brendan on his voyage to the Promised Land, and the whale, Jasconius, provided his back for Brendan's boat to rest on. In effect, what all these stories reveal is that the animals often became a significant part of the saints' daily lives, and important members, along with the human monks, of the monastic community itself.

As we look back, then, over the stories of saints and creatures in fellowship, a pattern already alluded to can be discerned: one of *reciprocity* that transcends species-differences so that all benefit in the circle of life. Kindness, compassion, loving respect on the part of the saints elicits from their creature-partners trust, caring, and love—which, in turn, increases the happiness of everyone. We have but to recall the story of Columban, the great Irish missionary to France, Switzerland, and Italy, that tells how he would call to the creatures as he walked through the woods. "They would come at once to his call, and he would stroke them with his hand and caress them; and the wild things and the birds would leap and frisk about him for sheer happiness, jumping up on him as puppies jump on their masters." Even the squirrel "would come at his call from the high tree-tops, and the saint would take it in his hand and set it on his shoulder, and it would be running in and out of the folds of his cowl." The joy is certainly evident in this story, a happiness that is shared by the animals and the saint himself.

The question can be asked, however, if this sense of kinship translated into any of the early Celtic saints' dietary choices. Judging from the saints' lives as well as certain Celtic monastic Rules, the evidence is mixed. Columcille on Iona, as related earlier, evidently followed a vegan diet, and expected his monks to do the same. Brendan was vegan who "from the time of his ordination to the priesthood tasted nothing in which the spirit of life drew support from flesh." David of Wales, according to his hagiography, rejected wine, beer, and everything intoxicating, "and led a blessed life for God on bread and water only." The daily diet of another saint, Finnian of Clonard (470–549 CE), consisted of "a bit of barley-bread and a drink of water," but on holy days "he would eat a slice of wheat bread and a piece of broiled salmon, and drink a full cup of clear mead or of ale."

Many monks, after these early saints, seem to have followed their example. In the latter half of the eighth century, Maelruain (d. 792 CE),

Conclusion

the founder of the Celi De reform movement, at his monastery of Tallaght, outside of Dublin, allowed only vegetables, a dry egg, cheese, and an occasional morsel of fish—but no meat—and no beer for most meals. "From the moment of his initiation into the clerical state," his Rule of Tallaght said, "a man did not eat the fat of bacon, or mutton, or venison or the meat of any other animal"—not even at the great celebration of Easter. At times, however, a monk could "content himself with salmon" (understandable, since it was *the* fish associated, for the Celts, with wisdom). In their admiration for the ascetic desert monks who had preceded them, early Celtic monks seem to have followed a highly restrictive diet. Some were vegan, while many others followed a vegetarian diet in which fish was allowed occasionally (Celtic monastic pescatarians?!). Whether their vegetarian or vegan diets were at all related to a respect for and compassion toward animals is difficult to know, but surely some, like Columcille and his decision to not allow any animals to be killed or eaten on Iona, did so as the result of their compassion and sense of interrelatedness—dimensions found in the stories of their saints.

Considering these stories of the saints, as well as their history of choices in their diets, what is it, then, that we might learn from them today in a world that is increasingly becoming, both East and West, more urbanized—and thus more removed from direct contact with nature and animals, wild or domestic?

From Patrick's protection of innocent deer when others wanted to kill them, we might challenge those who consider the hunting of ordinary as well as so-called trophy animals as a "sport," encouraging them to find other forms of recreation that do not involve the killing of fellow-creatures. From Brigit's concern for a terror-stricken boar and a flock of wild ducks, we might consider how animals are treated today in labs and factory farms, and the extreme cruelty and often prolonged suffering and terror they endure. From Columcille's decision that "the implement I bless will do no harm," we might work toward ending the slaughter of animals for food simply because we like the taste of meat. Maedoc's sympathy for a starving wolf might make us more attentive to our treatment of wolves today, often resulting in attempts at their annihilation. Kevin's patient care for a blackbird's nest and Melangell's for rabbits may induce us to start shelters ourselves or support them for birds and animals of all kinds. Even Godric has something to teach us about the treatment of those who are perceived as invaders to our gardens, inviting us to, yes, perhaps set up fences, but still to treat animals "kindly"—not destroying them for their simple desire to share our wealth.

Above all, the stories show how much our fellow-creatures can contribute to our own lives without having to give up theirs, so that we can all experience, like Columban, the shared joy of partnership. In response to this renewed awareness of our kinship with them, we too might reorient our lives, as many of the Celtic monks did, by choosing different approaches to our consumption of food, asking whether it is necessary for us to choose a vegetarian, if not a vegan diet.

All of this presupposes *a new spirituality of holiness* than that which has often been taught—and which increasing numbers of people, young and old, are rejecting, especially if raised in the Christian tradition. Instead of hearing that holiness is all about sexual continence and only a specific sexual orientation, the stories of the saints might remind us of the importance of developing an ethic of caring for creation in all its wondrous diversity. Instead of preaching or being lectured at on the importance of rules and respect for the hierarchy or elders, the example of the saints might rather teach the need for engaging in ministries of service and servant leadership. Instead of concentrating one's attention on the wealthy and the privileged, the saints' lives might affirm the importance of attending to the poor, the neglected, the marginalized, and all those who suffer, human and otherwise.

In the development of this "new spirituality," we might learn from these stories of the Celtic saints, as well as the stories of Jesus, whose life they sought to imitate, that this really isn't all that new! Jesus, when he walked the earth, saw God's love and compassion reflected in a myriad of ways, from the lilies of the field to the birds of the air, and especially in the lives of all who are suffering (see Luke 13:34; Matt 6:26–34). He challenged his followers to incorporate that awareness into their daily lives. His life encourages the pursuit of loving all creatures great and small, beginning with the tiny, fragile, beautiful planet on which we all live. And, as his ministry was about alleviating suffering whenever he saw it, he calls us still to do the same, to see his face in suffering humans like ourselves, but also to see, as the Anglican theologian Andrew Linzey recommends, "the face of the Crucified in the faces of suffering animals."

History shows and these stories reveal, Celts, ancient and Christian, had a high regard for animals as teachers and guides, healers and soul friends. They considered animals in many ways equal to humanity, and in some ways superior in their awarenesses and sensitivities. The Celtic saints reflected that awareness in their lives and their spirituality. Their sense of kinship with all of creation, their awareness of the reciprocity and friendship that we can have with our fellow-creatures is perhaps best expressed in a ninth-century poem, written by an Irish monk about his cat:

> I and Pangur Ban my cat,
> 'Tis a like task we are at:
> Hunting mice is his delight,
> Hunting words I sit all night.
>
> Better far than praise of men
> 'Tis to sit with book and pen;
> Pangur bears me no ill will,
> He too plies his simple skill.
>
> 'Tis a merry thing to see
> At our tasks how glad are we,
> When at home we sit and find
> Entertainment to our mind.
>
> Oftentimes a mouse will stray
> In the hero Pangur's way;
> Oftentimes my keen thought set
> Takes a meaning in its net.

'Gainst the wall he sets his eye
Full and fierce and sharp and sly;
'Gainst the wall of knowledge I
All my little wisdom try.

When a mouse darts from its den
O how glad is Pangur then!
O what gladness do I prove
When I solve the doubts I love!

So in peace our tasks we ply,
Pangur Ban, my cat, and I;
In our arts we find our bliss,
I have mine and he has his.

Practice every day has made
Pangur perfect in his trade;
I get wisdom day and night
Turning darkness into light.

May each of us, with the help of our animal teachers and guides, turn darkness into light, learning and sharing wisdom with all our fellow-creatures.

BIBLIOGRAPHY

Alexander, Dominic. *Saints and Animals in the Middle Ages*. Rochester, NY: Boydell Press, 2008.

Armstrong, Edward. *Saint Francis: Nature Mystic*. Berkeley: University of California Press, 1973.

Atherton, Mark. *Hildegard of Bingen: Selected Writings*. London: Penguin Books, 2001.

Barstow, Anne Llewellyn. *Joan of Arc: Heretic, Mystic, Shaman*. Lewiston, NY: Edwin Mellen Press, 1986.

Buechner, Frederick. *Godric*. New York: HarperCollins, 1980.

Carey, John, Máire Herbert, and Pádraig Ó Riain, eds. *Saints and Scholars: Studies in Irish Hagiography*. Dublin: Four Courts Press, 2001.

Chadwick, Nora. *The Age of the Saints in the Early Celtic Church*. London: Oxford University Press, 1961.

Charbonneau-Lassay, Louis. *The Bestiary of Christ*. New York: Parabola Books, 1991.

Charles-Edwards, T. M. *Early Christian Ireland*. Cambridge, UK: Cambridge University Press, 2000.

Colgrave, Bertram, trans. *Two Lives of Saint Cuthbert*. Cambridge, UK: Cambridge University Press, 1985.

Davies, Marion. *Sacred Celtic Animals*. Chieveley, England: Capall Ban Publishing, 1998.

Davies, Oliver, trans. *Celtic Spirituality*. New York: Paulist Press, 1999.

Duckett, Eleanor. *The Wandering Saints*. London: The Catholic Book Club, 1959.

Dumville, David, ed., and Kathleen Hughes. *Church and Society in Ireland, A.D. 400–1200*. London: Variorum Reprints, 1987.

Flower, Robin. *The Irish Tradition*. Oxford: Clarendon Press, 1947.

Follett, Westley. *Celi De In Ireland: Monastic Writing and Identity in the Early Middle Ages*. Woodbridge, UK: Boydell Press, 2007.

Ginnell, Laurence. *The Brehon Laws*. London: T. Fisher Unwin, 1894.

Gougaud, Dom Louis. *Christianity in Celtic Lands*. Dublin: Four Courts Press, 1992.

————. *Modern Research with Special Reference to Early Irish Ecclesiastical History*. Dublin: Hodges, Figgis & Co., 1929.

Green, Miranda. *Animals in Celtic Life and Myth*. London: Routledge, 1992.

————. *Symbol & Image in Celtic Religious Art*. London: Routledge, 1989.

Hood, A.B.E., ed. and trans. *St. Patrick: His Writings and Muirchu's Life*. London: Phillimore, 1978.

Jackson, Kenneth. *Studies in Early Celtic Nature Poetry*. Cambridge, UK: Cambridge University Press, 1935.

Johnson, Elizabeth. *Ask the Beasts: Darwin and the God of Love*. London: Bloomsbury Publishing, 2014.

Jonas. *Life of St. Columban*. Charleston, SC: BiblioLife, LLC, n.d.

Knox, David Blake. *The Curious History of Irish Dogs*. Stillorgan, Ireland: New Island Books, 2017.

Linzey, Andrew. *Animal Gospel*. Louisville, KY: Westminster John Knox Press, 1998.

————. *Why Animal Suffering Matters*. London: Oxford University Press, 2009.

Low, Mary. *Cherish the Earth*. Glasgow: Wild Goose Publications, 2003.

Mac Coitir, Niall. *Ireland's Animals: Myths, Legends, & Folklore*. Cork, Ireland: The Collins Press, 2010.

Matthews, John. *Celtic Totem Animals*. London: Connections Book Publishing, 2015.

McGinnis, Mark. *Buddhist Animal Wisdom Stories*. Boston: Weatherhill, n.d.

Bibliography

Meehan, Bridget Mary, and Regina Madonna Oliver. *Praying with Celtic Holy Women*. Liguori, MO: Liguori/Triumph, 2003.

Meyer, Kuno. *Ancient Irish Poetry*. London: Constable, 1994.

Murphy, Gerard. *Saga and Myth in Ancient Ireland*. Dublin: At the Sign of the Three Candles, 1955.

Olmsted, Garrett. *The Gundestrup Cauldron*. Vol. 162 of Collection Latomus. Brussels: Peeters Publishers & Booksellers, 1979.

Ó Maidin, Uinseann. *The Celtic Monk: Rules and Writings of Early Irish Monks*. Kalamazoo, MI: Cistercian Publications, 1996.

O'Meara, John, trans. *The Voyage of Saint Brendan*. Channel Islands: Colin Smythe Ltd., 1991.

Ó Riain, Pádraig. *A Dictionary of Irish Saints*. Dublin: Four Courts Press, 2012.

Plummer, Charles. *Lives of Irish Saints*, vol. 2. London: Oxford University Press, 1968.

———. *Vitae Sanctorum Hiberniae*, vol. 1. London: Oxford University Press, 1910.

Roberts, Holly. *Vegetarian Christian Saints*. Anjeli Press, 2004.

Russack, Neil. *Animal Guides: In Life, Myth and Dreams*. Toronto: Inner City Books, 2002.

Salisbury, Joyce. *The Beast Within: Animals in the Middle Ages*. New York: Routledge, 1994.

Schweitzer, Albert. *Civilization and Ethics*. London: Adam & Charles Black, 1946.

Scott, Michael. *Irish Animal Tales*. Dublin: Mercier Press, 1989.

Sellner, Edward. *The Celtic Soul Friend*. Notre Dame, IN: Ave Maria Press, 2002.

———. *Stories of the Celtic Soul Friends: Their Meaning for Today*. New York: Paulist Press, 2004.

———. *Wisdom of the Celtic Saints: Revised and Expanded Edition*. St. Paul, MN: Bog Walk Press, 2006.

Skinner, John, trans. *The Confession of St. Patrick*. New York: Image Books, 1998.

Stokes, Whitley, trans. *Lives of Saints from the Book of Lismore*. Oxford: Clarendon Press, 1890.

Thom, Catherine. *Early Irish Monasticism: An Understanding of its Cultural Roots*. London: T&T Clark, 2007.

Trask, Willard. *Joan of Arc: In Her Own Words*. New York: Turtle Point Press, 1996.

Waddell, Helen, trans. *Beasts and Saints*. London: Constable and Company, 1934.